Sacred Holidays

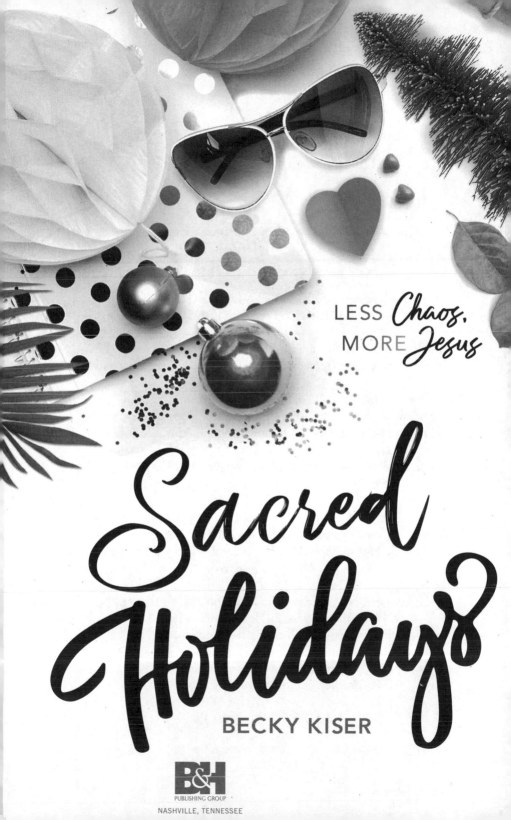

LESS *Chaos,*
MORE *Jesus*

Sacred Holidays

BECKY KISER

B&H
PUBLISHING GROUP
NASHVILLE, TENNESSEE

To Chris
You are my hero, best friend, and biggest cheerleader.
I choose you every holiday, and each day in between.
I love you. A lot a lot.

CONTENTS

HOW TO USE
THIS BOOK

BECAUSE IT'S DIFFERENT THAN OTHER BOOKS YOU'VE READ

Holidays can be crazy. And because you're holding this book in your hands, I think you'd agree. I love that about you—you are willing to face crazy head-on and do something about it. Holidays can be especially tricky to navigate as a Christian—wanting to celebrate and focus on Christ yet being pulled into the chaos or whimsy of each holiday.

You aren't alone; nearly every woman I talk to struggles with this. You don't have to stay in the same cycle of wishing things would be different. Jesus called us to not just live, but to live abundantly (John 10:10). This is the beginning of a new way of doing holidays—one that involves less chaos, more Jesus, and not getting too caught up in the holiday whimsy or magical festivities, nor overwhelmed by the holiday chaos.

I am so proud of you for getting this book! You're about to begin a journey to making holidays more sacred—holy and set apart! This book is laid out a little different than most books you've read before, so I wanted to walk you through how to use it.

WHAT THIS BOOK MEANS BY "SACRED"

Throughout this book, you'll hear me say a phrase over and over: "sacred—holy and set apart." Before we go any further, let me tell you what I mean by that phrase. I'm breaking up your approach to the holidays into two categories.

First, *holy*. I want to help your holidays become holy or *dedicated* to Christ (and others). Instead of getting lost in the way the culture does holidays (making it all about self or about applause you could receive for pulling off a perfect event), I want us to get lost in the reality that Christ gave us these holidays to enjoy, and that we can worship Him in the middle of all the whimsy. Even if a holiday isn't a direct celebration of Christ Himself, we can still put Christ and others at the center of all our celebratory moments instead of ourselves! While we don't want to over-spiritualize every single moment, sometimes we can be guilty of under-spiritualizing, can't we? Part of my mission in this book is to help you find more Jesus in each holiday, making it more holy for you, your family, and your friends.

Second, *set apart*. While we certainly want to make the holidays more about Jesus, we don't have to believe the lie that spiritual means impractical. Sometimes we need help setting apart a holiday from the rest of the calendar year, making it special with intentional planning. The "set apart" portion of the holiday chapters are simply there to help you be more intentional about your holiday habits in really practical ways.

As you'll see in each of the chapters that deal with specific holidays, I give you ideas about both of these categories. If you struggle with following in the culture's footsteps and forgetting the spiritual side of the holidays, lost in a sea of Pinterest activities and exhaustion, you'll see some ideas on how to make your holiday more holy, helping you get more Jesus! On the flip side, if you struggle with over-spiritualizing the holidays to the point of never even getting to practical ways of having fun, you'll also see some fun ideas on how to make your holiday "set apart" from the mundane of everyday life with whimsical activities and intentional plans. Sometimes during the crazy of celebration seasons, we need to pull away for more Jesus. Other times we need to bust out the planner, take the bull by the horns, and get intentional about our holiday planning so that we can look back and say it was truly set apart from the rest of the year in practical and fun ways. This book doesn't make you choose; it will help you make your holidays more holy *and* set apart.

THIS BOOK IS MEANT TO STAY OUT

I don't mean stays out in that pile of books you hope to read that crowd up your nightstand, taunting you from your shelves, unread. This book is one you keep within easy reach because you will want to reference it throughout the year. This book of yours is meant to be a companion that guides you through all holidays—not just the big ones. If we can change how we approach the holidays, our lives will be so much more free and full—and headed toward abundant living!

This past year I started keeping my planner on the counter, opened to the current day. By placing my planner out where I could see it each day, it radically changed my perspective on all the things I was juggling. I felt less overwhelmed and more in control than ever. I approached life with more intention and reached more goals than I ever could have imagined. I was able to say no to more things because I was able to see that I simply could not make them fit. I became a better follower of Jesus, wife, mom, friend, teacher, writer, boss, and neighbor. Don't get me wrong, I still have a long way to go. But this simple step of putting my planner out was a game changer.

What if you did the same thing with your holidays? What if instead of waiting to think about them right before they happen, or regretting afterward that you didn't approach them with more intention, you were prepared a month or two in advance? Let's stop living life in survival mode, constantly on the defense, a victim of our schedules and the expectations of others. Instead, let's live sacred—holy and set apart—with our holidays having less chaos, and more Jesus.

THIS BOOK IS MEANT TO BE READ IN STAGES

This book is broken up into three sections:

PART 1: LESS CHAOS, MORE JESUS

(READ RIGHT AWAY)

I know you want to quickly get to the meat of this book, the holiday chapters, where you'll receive practical insights for how you can make your holidays sacred. However, we must deal with our heart and our approach to holidays first. This section is to help set the stage for what it truly means to have less chaos and more Jesus during the holidays. Make time to read these two chapters before you begin the holiday chapters.

Before we get busy "doing," I want to remind you about the story of Mary and Martha in Luke 10. I think sometimes Martha gets a bad rap from her interaction with Jesus inside her home. Oftentimes she is portrayed as this frantic, bitter, workaholic woman, and the truth is, we just don't know that about her character. Sometimes I wonder if she was just like you and me—simply wanting to serve others and Jesus. Like her, we want to create this culture and way of life that brings God glory and others lots of joy. However—and this is a big however—we get lost in our doing and we just need to stop. Mary stopped and was found simply sitting at Jesus' feet, listening to what He had to say. Then we learn the real problem with Martha wasn't that she was serving but that she was *distracted* in her serving (v. 40). Jesus replied in verses 41–42, "Martha, Martha, you are anxious and troubled about many things, but one thing is necessary. Mary has chosen the good portion, which will not be taken away from her."

In Part 1 we will focus on the good portion before we focus on the tasks of carrying things out. Obviously, Martha had to work or else no one would eat. The problem wasn't in her working; it was in being so distracted she missed the good portion. Let's not miss it by being so distracted in our attempts to make holidays sacred. Let's first sit, listen, and learn. Then we can set the table and make the meal, but let's not be distracted by those first.

PART 2: HOLIDAYS

(READ 30–60 DAYS BEFORE HOLIDAYS)

You can certainly read Part 2 right away, but 30–60 days prior to each holiday, refer back to this section in order to receive the most continual benefit. Here you will find the following in each chapter:

- Encouragement in living sacred during this holiday.
- A little historical—cultural and/or religious—context.
- Write your personal mission statement or hope for that holiday.
- Ideas for all women to live sacred during each holiday.
- Ideas for the kiddos in our lives to live sacred too. *(Note: this isn't just for moms; see the section below to be reminded that this book is for every type of person, single, married, with kids, or otherwise, not just parents!)*
- Journaling space for you to record what's worked and what hasn't worked.
- Journaling space for you to record any ideas you can try in the future.

Go ahead and schedule your alerts on your calendar to prepare for each holiday. Set them as an annual recurring event. If you aren't able to make that appointment to plan, then commit to reschedule it for a better time. Since you are scheduling your holiday prep-time a year or more in advance, you will have to make adjustments. However, a simple reminder will increase the chances that you will make the time to sit down.

Check the box below after you've put the session on your calendar for each holiday:

- ❑ New Year's (schedule in November or December)
- ❑ Valentine's Day (Schedule in December or January)
- ❑ Lent and Easter (Schedule in January or February)
- ❑ Summer (Schedule in April or May)
- ❑ Halloween (Schedule in August or September)
- ❑ Thanksgiving (Schedule September or October)
- ❑ Advent and Christmas (Schedule in October or November)
- ❑ Happy Birthday (Schedule in _____)

PART 3: COMMON STRUGGLES

(READ AS NEEDED)

Finally, decide which common struggles you would benefit from reading. You might find it helpful to read through each of those chapters now, so you've learned what they have to teach you. Then come back to them as a refresher before the holidays hit. Know that your needs for each of these chapters will change year after year, hence the reason to keep this book within easy reach at all times.

THIS BOOKS IS MEANT TO GET MESSY

This resource was written for interaction. I view it as part book/part resource, in hopes that you no longer have to search the Internet for hours and hours to try to find what may or may not work for you. I have included some of the best practices for holidays—both the internal processing and prep that you'll find in Part 1 and in each of the holiday chapters from Part 2. However, there are many opportunities for you to process things out in this book. I will give you prompts and ask you questions, providing space for you to answer. Use this space; don't keep your pages clean. The more you interact with this book and make it your resource, the more sacred—holy and set apart—your holidays will become.

I have a sign that hangs at the bottom of my stairs that reads, "Pardon the mess but my children are making memories." I have it hanging there as a joke for others to read before they enter the war zone that can be our upstairs family room and my girls' shared bedroom. No matter how hard we try to clean or how many chore charts I hang, that space is always a mess. That sign reminds me each time I go upstairs that the messes are memories that my girls are making. I don't want them to live in a home with plastic coverings over our furniture or dishes they are afraid to touch. I want them to live in our home and make a ton of memories in it.

I have the same hope for you, my friend. This book is yours and I want you to make a mess with it. The more messes you make in it, the more memories you will have.

THIS BOOK IS MEANT FOR EVERYONE (NOT JUST PARENTS!)

I was very hesitant to include ideas for kids in this book for two reasons. First, I didn't want any person who wasn't a parent to feel like this book wasn't for them. It is so for you! It is for every person. The truth is, most of us have kids in our lives in some capacity—we are aunts, teachers, volunteers, grandparents, friends with moms, etc. These ideas I list are for anyone with a kid in their life, which is pretty much anyone! The hope is that we will all find ways to help train up children to have a more sacred approach to the holidays.

Second, I do not want parents to make holidays all about their kids. This is probably the number one question I get with Sacred Holidays, the ministry: "How can I help my kids learn more about Jesus during the holidays?" I love the heart of these parents so much, and I so get it. And as a ministry leader, I know I could be far more "successful" if I were to monopolize on this desire. The problem is, even though the intent is beautiful, the approach can be imbalanced. The best analogy I have for this is how the flight attendant says that we must first put our oxygen masks on and then help the child. For our children to have the best chance at life, we must first take care of ourselves. This is hard for us as moms because we will do just about anything for our kids. However, and this is a really big however, our goal is not to raise little Christian robots; our aim is to make disciples of Christ. But every disciple needs a discipler, someone showing them the way, not just telling them what to do (or programming their robot to do the right thing). We must show our kids the way by living the sacred way ourselves.

This book is a timeless resource for you, regardless of what season of life you find yourself.

THIS BOOK IS MEANT TO BE
EXPERIENCED ALONGSIDE OTHERS

We can't force others to change their approach to holidays, and that is never our aim. However, we can invite others on the journey toward making our holidays sacred—holy and set apart. The truth is, most of your friends and family members want the same thing you do! They want less chaos. And if they are believers, they want more Jesus too! If they are not, they probably do want the abundant life Jesus could offer through the holidays, but they simply have been searching for solutions in the wrong places. Christian or not, they all want to feel like they are living abundantly during the holidays, not caught up in the whimsy and survival-mode-crazy of it. So let's invite them to join us.

We know that we do better when we do things with others—there is power in numbers. It's the reason why weight-loss programs and workout places that promote group gatherings and accountability models are so successful. When we have others who are trying to make the same kind of changes we are, we do better.

We learn from their ways—what has worked and not worked. We have accountability to follow through. We discover more fun or efficient ways of doing things. We hear "me too" instead of assuming we're the only ones struggling with something. Plus, it's just a whole lot more fun!

Who are some people you could invite on this journey with you?

Send them a text message telling them what you are doing and invite them to join you! Put a check next to their name or cross it off once you've reached out to them.

Also, be sure to check out the Sacred Holidays website (sacredholidays.com) for other ways to build connection and community with our tribe of people, plus our team.

ARE YOU READY?

Okay, let's do this! Let's find less chaos and more Jesus in the holidays ahead! Let's make your holidays more sacred—holy and set apart. And let's find some freedom from common struggles that get the best of us too often.

We'd love to hear from you if you're on board, so we can follow along with your journey and our whole tribe can learn from you (our own virtual group). As you learn things or try things, be sure to tag @sacredholidays and use #sacredholidays in your posts, so we can all learn from and celebrate with one another. We are in this together!

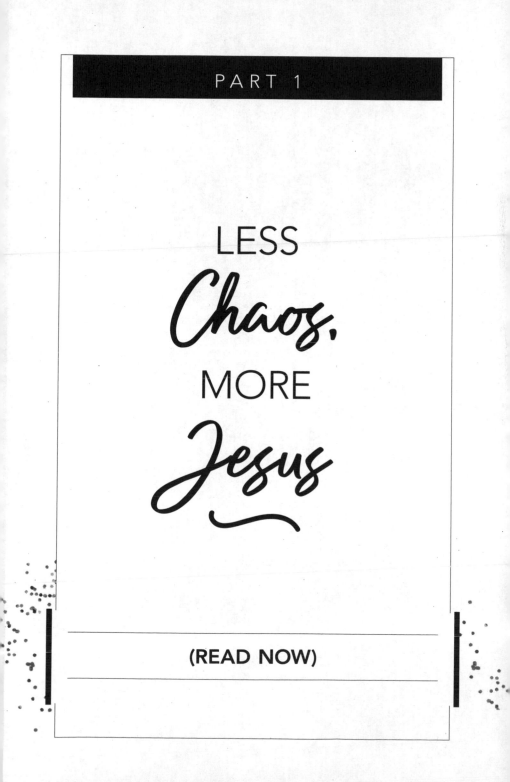

PART 1

LESS *Chaos,* MORE *Jesus*

(READ NOW)

CHAPTER 1

REGRETS, BETTER WAYS, AND BABY STEPS

This is the beginning of a new way for you—a new season of making holidays more sacred—holy and set apart. You should be really proud of yourself that you are taking the time to learn about this and actually making some changes. It's worth it; I can promise you that right now. This will not be easy, but, friend, it is so worth it and you can do this.

How many times have we talked to older women and heard, "I wish I would've done or known that when I was your age"? Let's learn from the women who are ahead of us and choose a different way, the one they wish they would've chosen (the one that still isn't too late for you, if you would consider yourself to be the older woman). We can choose this way when we are twenty-two, thirty-six, forty-four, fifty-nine, sixty-seven, and older. We are never too old for this! Let's not live a life of wishing we would've done something. Starting today, let's live the life we were meant to live—free from regrets and taking one baby step at a time toward a better way!

Holidays have become this imbalanced juxtaposition of chaos and whimsy. We are stressed by the shopping and thrilled by the look on the faces of the ones we spoiled. We are exhausted by the parties yet so excited to get all dressed up to celebrate the day or the person. We are easily irritated by our families and absolutely smitten at the same time. We hate ourselves for eating more than we should yet cannot get enough home cooking and treats. And we're torn between our love for all things whimsical and our deep desire to celebrate Jesus in each of the holidays.

The last one is the hardest, wouldn't you agree? We love Jesus and want to follow Him, yet we struggle to make the holidays about Him. We are stuck doing things the way they've always been done. We are stuck celebrating just as the world celebrates. We are stuck celebrating the way our family has always done it before or the way picture-perfect posts on social media have told us to over the years. The idea of something new, even something sacred, feels a bit overwhelming.

REGRETS

We all have regrets when it comes to the holidays, and oftentimes it's the shame of these regrets that keeps us from thinking we are even capable of a better way.

My biggest regret during all the holidays is how I inevitably default to the thirteen-year-old version of myself. When it was New Year's, I used to set big (and unrealistic) goals for myself, resolutions that lasted all of a week. On Valentine's Day, I was more concerned about who was showing me love than loving others (and chocolate, really it's about the chocolate). During Easter, it seemed to be more about the dress (priorities!). Summer can be a whirl of trying to have as much fun as possible. Halloween feels like a slightly rebellious thing to participate in as a Christian. Thanksgiving is the physical proof I turned thirteen when I'm surrounded by every member of my family. Christmas, while a celebration of Jesus' coming, can easily be overshadowed by wish lists and events. And my birthday never quite seems to measure up to the expectation in my head.

I'm a mess. We all are. We feel like we should have it all figured out by now and don't understand why we don't.

What Regrets Surround These Holidays?

Ask your Father to remind you of holiday-related regrets. Give yourself time to really process this today. Then, remember that this is your book, your resource for years and years to come. So come back to this page each year and you can add to the list below. The reason why we want to name the regrets is because we want to clearly and specifically identify the things we do not want to continue. There is no shame in naming it. (Tip: be general only when it's referring to someone else. Sometimes it's best to just use the first letter of a name or a place, to keep this page confidential.)

NEW YEAR'S:

_____

_____

VALENTINE'S DAY:

_____

_____

LENT AND EASTER:

_____

_____

SUMMER:

_____

_____

HALLOWEEN:

_____

_____

THANKSGIVING:

_____

_____

ADVENT AND CHRISTMAS:

_____

_____

HAPPY BIRTHDAY (INCLUDING YOUR BIRTHDAY AND OTHERS):

_____

_____

BETTER WAYS

We women are masters at staying in shame longer than we should, but shame has never been ours to carry. I'm a total word nerd and absolutely love the dictionary (and translation dictionaries). _Merriam-Webster's_ dictionary defines shame as "a painful emotion caused by consciousness of guilt, shortcoming, or impropriety. A condition of humiliating disgrace or disrepute. Something that brings censure or reproach; something to be regretted."

We just made a long list of regrets, which can tempt us to fall right back into that trap of shame, leading to guilt. We are vastly aware of our shortcomings. Holidays are so sweet and so magical in so many contexts, but we have so many regrets. So we settle into shame and believe there is no better way.

Before we move on to a better way of approaching the holidays, we must clearly identify what is true and what is a lie. What is true is all the things you listed above. We all have regrets about past holidays—wishing that certain elements were different. Identifying each one helps us learn. But the lie becomes evident when we take on shame, which isn't from your Father in heaven. John 8:44 speaks into this concept, "He [the devil] was a murderer from the beginning, and does not stand in the truth, because there is no truth in him. When he lies, he speaks out of his character, for he is a liar and the father of lies."

The father of lies, Satan, slithers right up next to the list of regrets we just processed and tells you, "Things will never change." He leads you to believe you will never get this right. He reminds you of others who have it all together (at least on their social media feed) and puts you in your place. He even tells you what a failure you are for not worshiping Jesus more during the holidays—holidays that are supposed to be about Him. He is the one who puts fear in us around holidays like Halloween or Christmas, causing more fear of the world than a love for others. Being a follower of Jesus in this day is so very complicated, and the enemy is taking every opportunity to slither up next to us and whisper lies in our ears, just as he did to Eve in the garden (Gen. 3).

When we look at our list of regrets above, we can listen to one of two voices: the voice of truth or the voice of lies. Jesus said in John 10:10, "The thief comes only to steal and kill and destroy. I come that they may have life and have it abundantly." I love how *The Message* translation by Eugene Peterson words this verse, "I came so they can have real and eternal life, more and better life than they ever dreamed of."

Yes! Isn't this what you want, my friend? Isn't this why you picked up this book? You believe there is a better way. You believe there must be a way "more and better than you ever dreamed of."

A New and Better Way

Just as we listed our regrets about the holidays, I want you to make a new and "better way" list. This list depicts what could be—and dreams about what you wish and hope would happen during the holidays. Don't over-spiritualize this either. Keep the traditions and cultural whimsy that are good and life-giving. Then ask your Father what might be a better way.

NEW YEAR'S:

_____

_____

VALENTINE'S DAY:

_____

_____

LENT AND EASTER:

_____

_____

SUMMER:

_____

_____

HALLOWEEN:

_____

_____

THANKSGIVING:

_____

_____

ADVENT AND CHRISTMAS:

_____

_____

**HAPPY BIRTHDAY (INCLUDING YOUR
BIRTHDAY AND OTHERS):**

_____

_____

I wish I could sit across from you now and hear these dreams God is creating in you. I know our tendency is to buffer our dreams just in case they don't come about. Here is what I want to encourage you to do, sweet friend: dream without the safety net. Abundant life in Jesus, as we defined earlier, is "more and better than they (that's you!) ever dreamed."

One of my favorite verses in all the Scriptures is the reality check that He is God and we are not, that is found in Isaiah 55:8–9, "For my thoughts are not your thoughts, neither are your ways my ways, declares the LORD. For as the heavens are higher than the earth, so are my ways higher than your ways and my thoughts your thoughts." Our Father takes such delight in our dreams and our faith. The reason why I love dreaming and planning is because it's part of the first steps of faith; it's our acknowledgment that there is actually a better way.

Then our Father takes it from there. He took Noah's first step and used him to build an ark. He took Moses—yes, the fearful-and-afraid-to-speak Moses—and used him to free the Israelites and part an entire sea. He used Esther, from the least favored lineage, to change a king's mind and save her people. He used David, the smallest of all his brothers, to kill the giant Goliath and become a king after God's own heart. He used John, a common fisherman, to be His most beloved disciple and be an elder to the early church for decades. He used Paul, a former persecutor and murderer of Christians, to be a major leader for the first followers of Jesus and writer of much of the New Testament letters.

We invite God into the dreams we hold in open hands, as we walk into each of these holidays asking and expecting Him to bring about a better way—one that is so much greater than anything we could ever imagine. We take the first steps, and He leads the path.

BABY STEPS

As I talk to women about making holidays sacred, I see it in their eyes: to change course feels so very overwhelming. Where do you even start? You start in one place and you pick one thing.

I'm an extremist, so I really struggle with this whole baby-step concept. I'm that person who is either 5 percent or 155 percent in. My closest friends and family know to never play a practical joke on me because I don't know how to respond without taking my reciprocal practical joke too far. It's one of the biggest pet peeves about myself, and most hilarious quirks. I have a really hard time with the whole "slow and steady wins the race" mentality.

So when I decided to change course with holidays many years ago, it was a little overwhelming, which kept me from doing anything. Actually, Pinterest kept me from doing anything because they had one million suggestions about everything. It took one search of the word *Advent* on Pinterest for me to quickly resolve to keeping things just as they had always been. And on that Christmas Eve, as I stood there with so many regrets, I knew I missed what was best because I stayed in ignorance, giving in to all-things overwhelming.

Let's not waste another year because these first steps seem too hard.

The very best thing you can do is "baby step" this process. I recommend that you choose one to three things each year and implement that. Get a strong foundation around that tradition and see how it works for you, then the next year implement the following thing. We will walk together through each of the holidays; plus you will create additional references to use for years to come. So all those awesome ideas you hear from others or see on Pinterest, if it inspires without making you crazy, you can jot those down in this book.

Doesn't that sound like a relief? Pressure is off, my friend.

Except there are a few of you who are stubborn and want all the change now. I get it; remember, I'm a fellow extremist. For any woman who has ever gone on a diet (which is most all of us), we know this—you can't lose all the weight on the first day. You can't even lose all the weight in the first month. Those who do lose weight quickly, typically gain most, all, or more back just as quickly because nothing really changed. Those who keep it off are the ones who slowly learned how to change their habits. We are also doing slow, committed change. I know that's not at all what you want to hear, but I wanted to lay all the cards on the table now. We can imagine that by the time we've turned the last page of this book that everything will be better. That we will have magically transformed holidays. I want to say I wish that was true, but I won't. The work is the refining part and it's the beautiful part of the journey too . . . even if it just so happens to be the most annoying part.

When I started working toward losing weight with my nutritionist, Amber, do you know how we started? That's right, one baby step at a time. Week one my goal was to start eating breakfast. I mean, how silly is that? I'm a grown woman—it should be assumed that I can handle eating breakfast. It shouldn't have to be an assignment that includes talking to a nutritionist for an hour and taking an entire week to work on. That is shame, and we already addressed shameful thoughts. So for a week I focused on breakfast. We made a list of three go-to healthy breakfast options. I committed to eat before my kids woke up, since that was one of my issues was not eating until all kids were up, taken care off, off to school, or down for naps. I put myself last and forgot about the basics. Shame kept me from realizing this. Do you know what week two homework was? To start my day with hot tea, instead of three cups of coffee. Ugh, I know. I almost stopped this whole thing. We talked through the benefits of starting your day with hot tea first. So I do that now; I start my day with hot tea, then breakfast, and then I have coffee. She knows that coffee is one of the great loves of my life and that wasn't something I was going to give up, so we kept it. Each week we continued doing one thing and because of that, I'm still doing it all these months later. This hasn't been an extreme change, but a gradual one.

This, my sweet friend, is what I want you to consider doing. It will feel painfully slow at first. However, in five years, ten years, and decades from now when you've reset your entire holiday culture for yourself, your family, and, likely, much of your community, you will be glad you took baby steps instead of sprinted and quit.

Just like my nutritionist let me keep the things I loved, like coffee, I want you to do the same—keep the parts you love, take out the parts that aren't healthy, and add in the things that would make it a "better way." Making holidays more sacred doesn't mean we become one of *those* Christians. You know the type, and we will talk more about them at the end of the book.

FEAR NOT, FOR I HAVE

To close out this chapter, I want you to read Isaiah 43, keeping in mind everything we've discussed: your regrets, His better way, and the baby steps you are about to take. This chapter in the Bible is one of the most life-giving chapters for me and I hope it wildly encourages you. Don't skip this part; take the time to slowly read through it.

As you read, ask your Father to heal the regrets, silence the shame of the enemy, show you a better way, give you the courage and faith to take the next baby steps, and for an increased trust that He will lead you and that He is able. I'm going to encourage you often to write in this book to make it the most awesome holiday resource you've ever had.

- Read through this Scripture once and just hear it.
- Then read it again and circle all the references of God (His name or reference to Him in any context).
- Then read it one last time and underline all the actions He has done, is doing, or will do (for example, in verse 1 you would underline the words "created" and "formed").

But now thus says the LORD, he who created you, O Jacob, he who formed you, O Israel: "Fear not, for I have redeemed you; I have called you by name, you are mine. When you pass through the waters, I will be with you; and through the rivers, they shall not overwhelm you; when you walk through fire you shall not be burned, and the flame shall not consume you. For I am the LORD your God, the Holy One of Israel, your Savior. I give Egypt as your ransom, Cush and Seba in exchange for you. Because you are precious in my eyes, and honored, and I love you, I give men in return for you, peoples in exchange for your life. Fear not, for I am with you; I will bring your offspring from the east, and from the west I will gather you. I will say to the north, Give up, and to the south, Do not withhold; bring my sons from afar and my daughters from the end of the earth, everyone who is called by my name, whom I created for my glory, whom I formed and made."

Bring out the people who are blind, yet have eyes, who are deaf, yet have ears! All the nations gather together, and the peoples assemble. Who among them can declare this, and show us the former things? Let them bring their witnesses to prove them right, and let them hear and say, It is true. "You are my witnesses," declares the LORD, "and my servant whom I have chosen, that you may know and believe me and understand that I am he. Before me no god was formed, nor shall there be any after me. I, I am the LORD, and besides me there is no savior. I declared and saved and proclaimed, when there was no strange god among you; and you are my witnesses," declares the LORD, "and I am God. Also henceforth I am he; there is none who can deliver from my hand; I work, and who can turn it back?" Thus says the LORD, your Redeemer, the Holy One of Israel: "For your sake I send to Babylon and bring them all down as fugitives, even the Chaldeans, in the ships in which they rejoice. I am the LORD, your Holy One, the Creator of Israel, your King." Thus says the LORD, who makes a way in the sea, a path in the mighty waters, who brings forth chariot and horse, army and warrior; they lie down, they cannot rise, they are extinguished, quenched like a wick: "Remember not the former things, nor consider the things of old. Behold, I am doing a new thing; now it springs forth, do you not perceive it? I will make a way in the wilderness and rivers in the desert. The wild beasts will honor me, the jackals and the ostriches, for I give water in the wilderness, rivers in the desert, to give drink to my chosen people, the people whom I formed for myself that they might declare my praise." (Isa. 43:1–21)

We silence those whispers of shame over our regrets with truth—His truth. It's simply not about us or our efforts; it's always been about Him. I hope you were in awe as you circled all those references about Him and underlined all He has or will do.

I want to wrap up this chapter by praying over you, my new friend:

Jesus, would You help my sister to believe this is all true of her. Silence, in the name of Jesus, all those lies of the enemy and accusations she hears from the regrets she has over past holidays. Free her from carrying that any longer. Give her a greater determination to change course than she has ever had before. Help her to desire and believe that there is a better way, more than any thought she could dream or way she could plan. You have said, Father, in Isaiah 55 that Your ways are higher. Help her to take the first step to higher, but keep her eyes fixed on You alone.

Lord, thank You for Your Word and all that Isaiah 43 showed us that You are. We proclaim, Father, that You are the creator of my friend, specifically formed by You. You are her redeemer. You have called her by name. By name, Father, You know and speak about her and to her! You call her "Mine"; she is Yours. You see her walking through the waters, and yet You are with her. You see her when she walks through the fire, and You keep her from being burned or consumed by the flames, even if she is surrounded by them. You say You are the Lord her God, the Holy One. You've exchanged so much for her. You see her as precious and honored and You love her. You don't want her to fear when You tell her You are with her, and You are Father—always with her. You speak in every direction and tell them what to give and want to withhold nothing from her. You've called her by name. You've created her for Your glory. You formed and made her just as she is. You call her Your witness. You say she is Your chosen servant all so that she would know and believe and understand that You indeed are Him, her Father. Would You help her to really know and fully believe and truly understand that You are Him! Lord, remind her that there has never been a God before or after You. Help her not to give her attention or belief to other gods or idols. Help her to know that You are the Lord and there is no one or no thing besides You that will ever save her. You are God. Your hand is faithful and

Your faithfulness is unchanging and reliable. You redeem her—taking what was and making it new. You are the Holy One over my friend, her Creator. You, Father, will make a way in the sea of her life, just as You made a way for Moses. You will cut the path for her—allowing all that she needs to pass. Help her not to dwell on former things, the regrets of the past holidays, or to even think about them. You, Lord, are doing something new! It's already starting! Help her to see it, feel it, and believe it! Remind her that You will make a way in her wilderness, all she doesn't yet see. You make rivers in the desert, taking what seems impossible and bringing not a way out but a way to sustain her as she makes her way through. Lord, You want her to praise You—give her the words to tell You and others how awesome You are!

Jesus, as she continues on through this book, would You lead her? Give her the space and determination to read this book and the discipline and courage to live it out. Surround her by community and family who will do this with her—a new way, a better way. In Jesus' name, I ask all these things. Amen!

CHAPTER 2

SOCIAL EXPERIMENTS AND ALL THINGS WHIMSY

I know what might be one of the things you are most concerned by, or at least what I was most concerned by: What will people think if I start to make changes and how will it affect them? I was on board personally but didn't want my girls or Chris, my husband, to feel like I had forced something on them. I didn't want our parents to be offended by us doing different traditions to infer that they did something wrong (because we loved holidays growing up). I was concerned that friends would think I was *that kind of Christian*; we will talk about *that kind* later on in the book, but you know the type. And I was really concerned how those who don't believe the same thing as I do would respond to me not doing things the "normal" way. I want so badly to be approachable and would hate to appear overly religious or pious because I choose a different way. I wanted to be able to express that I was still normal.

I wanted to love others well by learning about their traditions and celebrating with them, while still choosing what was best for my own family. The pursuit of learning and appreciating others, and yet still doing things differently for your own family, can be done in a healthy way. I just wasn't sure how to go about doing it.

I'm about to share a story with you, and I'm a little nervous to share it. Sharing something controversial this early in the book may make you want to shut this book and say, "No thanks." Please don't do that. Can I ask you one big favor? Will you finish this whole chapter? Don't roll your eyes or count me out until you have heard everything. Deal?

Doing things a different way and sharing that change with others is a hard part of the process; and, unfortunately, it's just not something you can avoid. I don't mean this to be glass-half-empty, but you will disappoint people regardless of what you choose. When we started making changes, we already had plenty of opinions, some spoken and some very loudly unspoken, on how we were already not doing things right. We will deal with expectations later in the book, but I wanted to touch on this now. You will always fail to meet the expectations you have for yourself and others have for you.

THE AWKWARD ANNOUNCEMENT

My journey into more meaningful holidays began with Advent, but as we will discuss in this book, it is not the only holiday that we can make sacred. It's just where I happened to begin.

I was a little unsure how others would react when I started making changes to the holidays. At first no one really noticed because so much of the change was an internal shift. The first year I was intentional about Advent and trying to focus on celebrating Jesus' coming, it really didn't change things for anyone else but myself. Then the next year my daughter was no longer an infant and had entered the toddler days, and we were faced with the question every parent asks: How are we going to do this "Santa" thing?

Our parents and friends were curious about several things: Would we wrap gifts from Santa or leave them unwrapped? Would he leave one gift or many gifts? How would we explain him getting in the house since we didn't have a fireplace? These are all the normal questions you ask.

The hard part came when we made the announcement to friends and family: we weren't doing Santa. "What do you mean you aren't doing Santa?" "You are going to ruin Christmas for them!" "Well, *we* did Santa and you turned out just fine." So many comments, interesting looks, and even more opinions.

OUR SOCIAL EXPERIMENT: ALL THINGS WHIMSY *AND* JESUS

My story starts with my kids, but those without kiddos in your life, don't check out. This is my story of where I started because it was my life at the time of my breakthrough. Your circumstances do not need to affect your intentionality to make your holiday sacred. You can do this if you live alone or with roommates, a spouse, or kids. You can do this if you are single, dating, divorced, married, or widowed. You can do this if you are unemployed, work part-time, work full-time, work from home, or travel a lot for work. You can start today.

This is my story of how I started. I wanted my kids to have a whimsical—winsome, sparkly, festive, full of fun, fanciful—holiday experience. What I had noticed is that Christmas was only truly magical for kids ages three to seven, and only for as long as they believed in Santa. After that, they played along for younger siblings or cousins, which is a strange mix of still totally fun and a bit disappointing. Then enter the teenage years and early twenties, and it just feels so different. You love the presents, of course, but the magic is pretty much gone. Then once you enter adulthood, older adults start to reassure you that you will experience the magic of it again when you have children. Then they all pass the age of seven, and the funk enters again, and you wait to be grandparents for the magic.

Here's what I didn't like: so much of the whimsy of Christmas was wrapped up in the magic of one man, Santa. Do you know the question my kids are asked about one billion times from friends, family, doctors, cashiers, waiters, and random strangers on the street: "What are you going to ask Santa to bring you for Christmas?" This made me cringe every single time. I wanted this time of year to be so much more for my kids than what they were going to be getting for Christmas under the tree.

I began to notice how much time it took to convince kids of this story and then equal amounts of energy to keep the magic of it all alive. I also felt like the holiday became more and more centered on the gifts, and this is true for adults too.

Don't get me wrong, the whole thing is so much fun, so very much fun. And kids and their families love Santa, for so many good memories (that we will talk about at the end of the book in the Santa chapter). My struggle wasn't in believing that. I love make-believe and I am constantly setting the stage for my girls to use their imaginations. My issue with it all wasn't so much the "lying" aspect.

What it came down to was this: I wanted to create magic and whimsy around something that wasn't contingent on one idea. I believed that my children didn't need to experience the holiday blues once the truth of Santa was revealed or if they didn't get every item on their wish list. I wanted to bring back the whimsy for myself, too, that my own love for Christmas wasn't contingent on the giggles of my girls as they strained to listen to Rudolph's hooves on our roof.

On top of all that, I knew that there was a significant spiritual piece to Christmas that I was missing—it was created for us to celebrate the coming of Jesus! And if I am honest, that was much more of an afterthought. Sure, we went to the Christmas program, Christmas Eve service, and at some point would try to read Luke 2. Other than those efforts, we hadn't really attempted much else to make this season a celebration of the One who had come.

So instead of focusing on the build up of Santa's arrival and all the gifts, we shifted focus. We teach our kids about St. Nicholas and why there is a Santa. We don't pretend that he is real but we honor him as a great example of how to live at Christmas time. His legacy of generosity is a beautiful one to celebrate this time of year. We go snap pics with Santa each year because we love what his legacy represents. Instead of focusing on the wish lists for ourselves, we focus hard on gift-giving and being generous. Last but truly not least, we intently focus on Jesus' coming. (I'll share more in detail about all of this and more in the Advent chapter.)

Advent was the starting point for me. It gave me the confidence and the insight to make changes to other holidays, one baby step at a time.

THE RISK AND THE RETURN

As I told those who challenged us, mostly out of love and concern for what our family would miss out on, with this approach, we don't know how this will go. Our girls could totally resent us one day for robbing them of the magic of Santa. If I'm honest, this is a big fear of mine. It's one thing to do a social experiment on ourselves, but to potentially rob our kids of this, I was super nervous.

Here is what I can tell you seven years into this experiment: our kids are ridiculously obsessed with the holidays. All of them, not just Christmas. I mean obsessed. My oldest writes about them during free writing time at school all year round. Just the other day she wrote me a thank-you note because she was so happy about how fun I make Christmas at our house and that she loves our house most of all at Christmas time. Listen, there are about a million things I've done wrong as a mom, and my kids are so far from perfect, but I can confidently tell you that we haven't messed them up by not doing Santa.

I share this so that you know you will have to take some social experiment risks of your own to get the return you are hoping to achieve. Christmas isn't the only holiday with risk associated with it by choosing to make the holiday sacred—holy and set apart—which is why we have included all the main holidays we all celebrate.

The return of taking these risks isn't to just make one holiday sacred, but to see all the other ones slowly begin to morph as well. And as that transformation happens year after year, you begin to reap the returns of the risks. You get confidence in telling others about your decision to change things.

It's not easy to take risks; in fact it's pretty scary. I still get a little anxious every time someone asks my kids about Santa. I still get nervous that friends and family will judge me a little for robbing my girls of the magic attached to him. But those concerns and insecurities are quickly overshadowed by the goal of what I am trying to achieve long term, both for me and my family.

We all only have a certain amount of time and energy to put toward things—we can choose what everyone else is doing or we can choose the sacred. One way is easy and keeps you at pace with the rest of the world but leads to consistent slumps year after year. The other way is different and uncomfortable, but it is focused on the greatest commandment: love God and love others.

A LOVE FEST

The Pharisees, the pious and religious elite, loved challenging Jesus. They wanted so very much to catch Him saying something He shouldn't, something that went against Jewish law, so that they had justification to arrest Him. In Matthew 22:37–39, Jesus was questioned by one of them about which command was the greatest. He said to them, "You shall love the Lord your God with all your heart and with all your soul and with all your mind. This is the great and first commandment. And a second is like it: You shall love your neighbor as yourself."

Our holidays should be consumed with asking ourselves if we are loving God and others well. Everything else, including treasured traditions and the opinions of others, is secondary. Secondary doesn't mean off-limits. This is why I have many friends who love God and others, while simultaneously doing the Santa thing with their kids. And their kids love Christmas at their house as much as my kids love Christmas at our house. It's just not about the details; it's about the love. On the flip side, there are families that do practice every religious tradition you could fathom, and yet there is no love. In their attempt at setting apart these holidays, they've removed the joy, love, and every bit of the whimsy.

There is much about our Father and His command to love Him and others that is not open for interpretation. As much as our culture likes to push the borders on biblical truth for the sake of cultural relevance, truth is truth. If we believe Him to be Lord, we must believe that His Word, every bit of it, is true. We don't get to pick and choose the parts that we like. There is a lot that is clearly defined about how we can best love God and others. However, there is much that is not defined in the Bible. What remains is left for us to uniquely express in our own lives, and in this case, like whether a Jesus-loving family does or does not do Santa. So when it comes to the holidays, we can move around various traditions with freedom.

Your Father is not one who wanted you to be like the Pharisees—consumed by keeping the law, so much so that you missed the love or the One who is love. Find your way with each and every holiday, keeping them both holy (dedicated to Christ and others) *and* set apart from the rest of the year (intentionally fun and memorable!).

JESUS LIKED A GOOD PARTY

When I used to work in the corporate world, many of my friends who didn't believe in or follow Jesus were determined to get me to do things that they knew were off-limits for me. I'm not sure why, but I think they liked the idea of corrupting the "good girl." Trust me, my story is so far from good. Grace is something I know so well. Needless to say, they were intent to see me go too far. Their favorite thing to say to me was, "Even Jesus liked a good party! His first miracle was turning water into wine." I give them an A for effort and an F in biblical context.

While I don't believe that Jesus' miracle of turning water into wine (Matt. 22) means that we should all get drunk, I do think there is a reason He chose this moment to begin His ministry. I also don't believe you need a degree or even a study Bible to understand Scripture, although those are excellent tools to better understand His Word. We aren't going to dive into the deep theological perspectives of this very controversial, first miracle. But we are going to look at it purely and simply with the first Bible study tool I learned: observation. When I was taught how to study the Bible, I was taught this process: observe, interpret, and apply.

What we know for sure of Jesus in this story is that He was at a wedding; He *chose* to attend a celebration.

A few things that I observe from this account are that when He was informed there was a problem that would affect the celebration, He helped provide for the celebration, He used what was common (water) to make something remarkable (according to the master), His glory was manifested, and this caused the disciples to believe.

While the holidays may not be the primary point of this passage, we can certainly use Jesus' example to help us engage in public celebrations. Whatever the celebration, what if you chose to show up? Once there, what if you sought to find a need and asked Jesus to help you provide for that need? What if, instead of feeling weird or left out—or fearful of people judging you—their eyes were opened when they saw that you turned something common into something remarkable? What if the way you engaged a public event or holiday had the power to open people's eyes to who Jesus is and how He works?

Friend, I have some really good news for you. Christ has already showed up at the celebration and if you believe in Him, then you are a part of Him! If you are present there, then *He* is present there, ready to minister! Second Corinthians 5:17 says, "If anyone is in Christ, he is a new creation. The old has passed away; behold, the new has come."

I know whatever social experiment you are about to do regarding holidays may feel a bit overwhelming at times. When it does, remember that you are in Christ and you are a new creation. When this rebirth occurred, He took what was old and made something new. You are new, and He is in you. And we are told that the old, all that *was*, has passed away when we were reconciled to God. And He has new things for us and new ways for us to engage those around us according to His example!

Let's not separate our holiday traditions and our cultural celebrations from this new life that He brings. Let's invite Him into our celebrations!

INVITE HIM IN AND SIT DOWN

One of the most common and relatable stories in Scripture during the holidays, especially for women, is the story of Mary and Martha. If you have been in church for a number of years, stay with me; I know you've heard this story one thousand times at women's events.

Our slogan at Sacred Holidays is "less chaos, more Jesus." We repeat that again and again for our people and include that hashtag on so many things we share on social media to remind ladies that we are going after less chaos and more Jesus. The problem is we are drawn to the chaos, like moths to the light. Most of us really struggle to sit still for very long. Or if we do sit still, it's less like Mary and more just lazy. However, Mary and Martha show us in Luke 10 that there is a drastic difference between being busy and resting.

Mary gets a lot of credit in this story for being the good, sweet sister who sat at the teacher's, at Jesus', feet. But have you ever noticed who actually welcomed Jesus into their home? It was Martha. Martha was available enough to invite Jesus in; she just got distracted serving Him. Can't we all relate to this story? We want so much to invite Jesus into all our holidays—and we do! Then we get so distracted serving Him and others that we miss Him altogether.

After complaining about her sister not helping, Jesus replied, "Martha, Martha, you are anxious and troubled about many things, but only one thing is necessary, Mary has chosen the good portion, which will not be taken away from her."

I love how Jesus said her name twice. We need that so often, a little snap back to reality to get our attention. He addressed her feelings—she was anxious and troubled about so much. Know that your Savior knows just how you are feeling about each of these holidays and all that they encompass for you. But He will always call it like it is, and for Martha, He knew she wasn't choosing the good way.

CHOOSE THE GOOD

That's what this book is all about—choosing the good portion, the better way! It won't be easy, we know that, but it will be good! The whimsy of each of these holidays isn't found in the details or the elaborate gestures; it is found in Jesus. When we make choosing Him a priority, we find the whimsy. And it's a whimsy that doesn't fade with age; it only increases.

It's your turn now to make the holidays your own social experiment, one baby step at a time. Remember that whimsy takes time, and it takes sitting down at the feet of Jesus and waiting for Him to work a miracle!

PART 2

Holidays

**(READ 30–60 DAYS
BEFORE HOLIDAY)**

CHAPTER 3

NEW YEAR'S

While there is nothing truly different between December 31 and January 1, the change from one year to the next feels like a giant fresh start. The previous year, with all its ups and downs, is behind us as we move on to uncharted territory.

I'm not sure how you feel about a new beginning, but fresh starts are my favorite! I am the girl who loves a clean slate. I loved a new school year or a new semester and getting all new school supplies. I loved mid-semester when I'd get OCD and rewrite my entire binder because it had gotten too messy. I love rearranging furniture to make a space feel new. I love going shopping or visiting a new place. I love all things new. There is something so exciting about uncharted territory. If you are like me, then you will love this chapter, and you'll likely have a lot to add to it in the sections at the end when you journal through ideas!

I know something new, particularly something unknown, isn't always appealing, especially when what's been was working out just fine for you. So I hope this chapter gives you some ideas that help you walk into this new year with confidence and hope. And remember, baby steps. We add in just one thing with the aim to make our holidays sacred—holy and set apart.

WHY DO WE CELEBRATE NEW YEAR'S?

This holiday isn't a specifically religious one, but it is definitely a holiday most people celebrate so I wanted to include it in this book. I hope this book helps you find ways to make all holidays, not just the religious ones, sacred—holy and set apart. There is nothing blatantly spiritual about a new year, but for me, it's one of the most spiritually awakening of all the holidays. It's a time for me to really connect with the Father to look back on what He has done, what I have done, and also to give thanks! It's a time to look ahead and ask for faith to dream the kind of dreams He has for me and set the kind of realistic and faith-filled goals to make those dreams happen. It's a season to reflect and ask the Father what things need to be removed from my life—sin, relationships, commitments, or physical things that are holding me back in some way.

I don't mean to over-spiritualize this holiday by sharing verses about new beginnings, but I want you to read through these to know your Father is about new things:

- Psalm 98:1–3: "Oh sing to the LORD a new song, for he has done marvelous things! His right hand and his holy arm have worked salvation for him. The LORD has made known his salvation; he has revealed his righteousness in the sight of the nations. He has remembered his steadfast love and faithfulness to the house of Israel. All the ends of the earth have seen the salvation of our God."
- Lamentations 3:22–24: "The steadfast love of the LORD never ceases; his mercies never come to an end; they are new every morning; great is your faithfulness. 'The Lord is my portion,' says my soul, 'therefore I will hope in him.'"
- Isaiah 40:30–31: "Even youths shall faint and be weary, and young men shall fall exhausted; but they who wait for the LORD shall renew their

strength; they shall mount up with wings like eagles; they shall run and not be weary; they shall walk and not faint."

- Isaiah 43:18–19: "Remember not the former things, nor consider the things of old. Behold, I am doing a new thing; now it springs forth, do you not perceive it? I will make a way in the wilderness and rivers in the desert."
- Ezekiel 11:19: "And I will give them one heart, and a new spirit I will put within them. I will remove the heart of stone from their flesh and give them a heart of flesh."
- 2 Corinthians 5:17: "Therefore, if anyone is in Christ, he is a new creation. The old has passed away; behold, the new has come."
- Ephesians 4:22–24: "To put off your old self, which belongs to your former manner of life and is corrupt through deceitful desires, and to be renewed in the spirit of your minds, and to put on the new self, created after the likeness of God in true righteousness and holiness."
- Colossians 3:9–11: "Do not lie to one another, seeing that you have put off the old self with its practices and have put on the new self, which is being renewed in knowledge after the image of its creator. Here there is not Greek and Jew, circumcised and uncircumcised, barbarian, Scythian, slave, free; but Christ is all, and in all."
- 1 Peter 1:3: "Blessed be the God and Father of our Lord Jesus Christ! According to his great mercy, he has caused us to be born again to a living hope through the resurrection of Jesus Christ from the dead."

I'm not sure if you've ever invited the Father into your New Year's traditions and goal setting, but I hope this is a new year, a new beginning, of making the year sacred from the very start!

WHY DO YOU CELEBRATE THE NEW YEAR?

Make Your Personal New Year
MISSION STATEMENT

Write out what you want the celebration of the New Year to be about (and not about). This is where you make what was just a holiday into a Sacred Holiday—holy and set apart. We will get to the details of how you will carry it out, but first start with what you want this season to be about.

IDEAS FOR A MORE SACRED NEW YEAR

Don't try to do all of these ideas or try to implement all the other ideas you've heard before. Take baby steps into each holiday. (Go back and read chapter 1 if you need this reminder.) Pick one or two things to try this year and do them really well. Make notes in the white spaces of what did and didn't work, so you have a customized resource for many years to come!

HOW TO MAKE NEW YEAR'S *HOLY*

Word of the Year and Realistic Goals

While most people start off the new year with a goal in mind, very few finish the year with that goal accomplished. This is why I'm not the biggest fan of resolutions, but I have loved choosing a word, or a phrase, from the Lord that guides my next year. I'm going to walk you through what I do each year, but the first thing you should know is be flexible, give yourself grace, and find the way that the Lord unfolds for you. This is meant to be a guide for you, but this is not the only way to go about setting goals. Use this as a starting place, then make it your own. This is what works for me. Alter this to work best for you.

FIRST: CHOOSE YOUR CATEGORIES

The first thing I do is divide my life up into categories. I do this by looking at the key spheres of my life that God has given me to steward. This will be different for each of us. For me that would be: wife (marriage), mom (parenting), spiritual life (walk with the Lord, service, church, etc.), work (speaking, teaching, writing, and Sacred Holidays), health/physical, and fun (this includes things like friendships, adventure, etc.).

> Grab a journal and list out the categories that best apply for you.

Remember these can evolve—you can always add categories, consolidate, and remove categories. Nothing needs to be set in stone. This is a starting place.

SECOND: FIND YOUR WORD (OR PHRASE)

The process to finding your word will look different for each person and might change each year. There are some years I've known what my word would be months before the new year. Two years ago, things were crazy out of order for me—we had just had our third kid, Sacred Holidays was growing, and life was becoming a bit too blurry. I don't believe in balance, but I love the idea of a healthy rhythm. So, I knew my word would be *rhythm*, to find a healthy and more consistent up and down to my life. Another year, my word for that year was *adventure* since the Lord revealed that I had been playing it too safe in some areas. In yet another year, I was going at the speed of light and needed to slow down. I share these examples to show you that there isn't one way to find your word or phrase. Your only job is to sit before the Lord and invite Him in the process.

> *Spend some time reflecting:*

- *Do you already know what your word should be? Write it down!*
- *Look at your year in reflection; does that help you determine what you should focus on?*
- *Still stuck? Maybe ask a friend or family member. Sometimes they can see our blind spots and potential better than we can.*

Again, give yourself time to find your word. We aren't bound by dates. You could find your word on January 1, January 6, or August 13. There is nothing that says we need to know for sure by January 1 what our word should be. The beauty of the new year is that it challenges us to set a new goal, to make a fresh start. But we are not bound to this one day. You aren't a failure if it is January 6 and you are just trying this. You aren't a failure if it is August 13 and you are starting this. Baby steps and lots of grace.

Also, don't get stuck on your word. Don't let this trip you up. You might need to skip to setting some goals to find your word. The purpose of having a word is it gives you a very clear aim that God would have you pursue for the year. It helps you remember and live with more intention. Instead of having a lofty goal or a list of goals, this gives you some cohesion and helps you have more attachment to your ambitions. But don't let the word trip you up.

THIRD: SET YOUR GOALS AND STICK WITH THEM

Once you know your word then you are ready to set some goals. Again, every personality might want to approach this differently. For me, I love dreaming what I'd love to accomplish for the year in each category. I dream big and push myself for this. Then I get realistic with monthly goals to make this happen. Most of us can set a goal for something a year out. The only way to make it happen is when we set realistic markers to get us to that big goal.

> *Where would you like to be a year from now within each of your categories?*

> *What can you do this month to take a realistic step toward your goal for the year?*

Start there. One step at a time. You always have the next year in mind, but all you really need to be concerned about is what you are aiming to accomplish this month.

This is the hardest part about setting goals, isn't it? We have the best of intentions and yet we struggle to stick with it. The way we stick with it is looking past the annual goal and breaking it down to one step at a time.

> *Break it down more—what do you need to do this week to meet your monthly goal?*

> *One more—what do you need to do today to meet your weekly goal?*

This is how we reach our goals, one day at a time. But there are a few other things we can do to really help us reach our goals.

> *Who can you invite into your goals to help hold you to it?*

Accountability is one of the best things we can bring into our lives. Give a few people permission to check in on you from time to time about this.

> *What alerts can you set to make sure you stick with it?*

Maybe you need to set an alarm for each morning to set your daily goals. Or maybe you set a monthly appointment on your calendar to go over your goals. The way we stay focused on our goals six months later is by focusing on our goals one month, week, and day at a time. Goals are only achieved with effort.

Turn Your Word or Goal into a Bible Study

This is my favorite part of the process of choosing a word for the year and one I hope helps you find freedom and greater achievement toward your goals. I always have a lot of people ask me for Bible study recommendations to do between Advent and Lent, and this is what I recommend—a word study on your word for the year. If you aren't familiar with word studies, it's a topical approach to studying Scripture. When there is a certain topic or issue that I want enlightenment on, or want to grow in, I love to look up Scriptures on that subject and then study them.

Below are some tips to approach your topical word of the year study. This isn't meant to be done in one sitting. Use the next month, or however long you need, to process through these steps. They will help you enjoy more of Jesus during the start of the year and ensure that your goals are in line with His Word the whole year through!

Here are some ways you can study your word in the Word:

- Use a concordance or online Bible tool to look up every verse that contains your word.
- Read through those verses and make note of the ones that resonate.
- Read the context of those verses that resonate and identify some that you feel particularly inspire or correct.
- Study those verses—what do they mean? What does this teach you about God? How should you apply them?
- Post them around places you pass often. I keep them on my bathroom mirror, above the water on my fridge, etc.
- Pray over these verses.

Reflect and Be Grateful

Take some time on New Year's Eve, New Year's Day, or that week to look back on the prior year. What were successes or wins? What were disappointments or failures? How are you grateful?

I know this time of year is all about looking forward, but there is great value in looking back too. Celebrate what Jesus has done, and worship Him. Then also take the time to learn from what didn't work so you don't walk into the new year with the same things tripping you up. Give this step time and space. This might take an entire week to do, or maybe just an hour.

Celebrate with Others

One thing we will see as a very sacred practice to every holiday is to gather with others. Community is something we see from the very beginning when God saw that Adam needed a helpmate, that it wasn't good for him to be alone (Gen. 2:18). As we read through the Old Testament, we see the Israelites celebrate, mourn, travel, worship, and so much more in the context of community. Jesus began His ministry by calling disciples to follow Him. Much of His life that we read about is spent with others. Then we witness the early church frequently gathering together, as well. Gathering is very much a spiritual thing, even if you are an introvert!

New Year's Eve is a beautiful day to gather with someone special or a big group of special someones to celebrate what is to come! Plan a day that would be meaningful and special to you and do that. As a follower of Christ, it might be hard for you to know how to celebrate this big without celebrating in the crazy ways you see the world celebrating. This is where you can be creative and choose to celebrate in a clean and fun way. When I first became a Christian in high school, this was super important to me. I didn't want to ring in the new year as I had in prior years, and I wanted to create a place that was more fun than all the parties others would throw. I was determined to prove that you could have fun without feeling regret. Our house became the place people came to for New Year's. One of my favorite traditions we began doing, spontaneously one year, was to begin a worship service at midnight. It was a powerful way to kick off the new year worshiping God with our house busting full of people.

Things have changed now that I have kids and I've had to shift my expectations of what New Year's can look like. With that said, since it is so easy for us to compare our lives to others with social media, do not let your year start off in the comparison trap. There will be some years your celebration is sequins and red lipstick, and other years it is flannel pajamas and fireworks on the TV. One does not make you more cool than another. Do what works for you. Do what brings you joy in Christ, and find ways to focus on others as you celebrate a new year.

Pray over Christmas Cards

As you pack away Christmas, leave out all the Christmas cards you've received that year to pray over them. There are several ways you can do this:

- Put all the cards in a pile and pray a blessing over everyone generally.
- Spend some time going through each card one more time and praying over each person or family.
- Leave them in a basket on your table all year long and every so often at dinnertime pull out a card and pray over that family before or after your meal.

A bonus to this could be to text, email, or call that person to let them know you've prayed over them, or that you are about to pray over them and ask for any specific requests.

Have a Family Worship and Prayer Night

On New Year's Day, or that week, set aside some time to pray for the upcoming year as a family. Use that time to pray over each child individually. Maybe even have a few songs prepared to play on your phone, if you aren't musically inclined, to sing together as a family.

HOW TO MAKE NEW YEAR'S *SET APART* FROM THE REST OF THE YEAR

These ideas aren't always overtly spiritual, nor do they have to be. They are simply ways you can make this holiday more intentional, memorable, and distinct during the year.

Get Rid of Things

I've already shared how I love fresh starts, and there is something so freeing about a new year as you put your Christmas decorations away and have a clean slate. Use this fresh slate to clean house a little more. Go through each room and closet and see what you can get rid of. If you haven't used it in the past year, chuck it or donate it. If it doesn't bring you joy anymore, let it bring joy to someone else and donate it. Schedule a day to finally tackle those spaces that have been cluttered and disorganized for some time.

Kids Party at 12 Noon

Including your kids in the celebration of the day is so fun, but so not fun if you try to do that at midnight. Throw a party for your kids at noon instead! This could be a really great way to reach out and get to know your neighbors too. So invite your kids into the planning process and use this as an opportunity to teach them about the value of community and celebration! If you don't have kids, but kids live in the neighborhood around you, offer to host something like this in your own home. This would let the surrounding adults in your community know that you are interested in their life and give you a great opportunity to get to know them.

Coaching Kids to Set Goals

If you have children, invite your kids into the goal-setting process too! This is a great way that we can disciple our kids. We know what a struggle setting realistic goals can be and how hard it is to stick with them. What a gift it would be to have started learning goal-setting as a child! A few things to remember:

- Encourage them to choose it (don't choose it for them). You may really want them to learn something or work on a certain character trait, but let this be their thing. You can certainly help them think through what are some things they want to start or stop doing. But let them pick the goal, which will help them be more motivated.
- Make sure it is age-appropriate and realistic. If you think it might not be, ask your child if they think that is something they could actually do or not do. Then talk through what that might look like to actually achieve it.
- Help them set small baby steps to achieve the main goal.
- Set up a monthly meeting with your child to go over the goals. This is a great time to reevaluate what baby steps are working and which ones need to be adjusted. They might even realize that this is a goal they really aren't motivated to do and you can help them find a new goal. Again, this is part of the coaching process in teaching them about sticking with goals and making new goals.
- Let your child know that you are their biggest fan and be just that! Encourage them when you see them working hard on their goal. Celebrate with them when they meet their baby-step goals and think of a way you can incentivize them along the way.

Set a Group Goal

Sit down with your roommates or kids and choose a goal of something you all want to do as a unit. Try to make the household goal something everyone wants to be working on and is excited about. You might want to come ready with several suggestions to help steer the ideas, but let your kids or roommates really own the goal as a whole. To help incentivize them (and yourself), decide as a group little rewards along the way for sticking with your goal. If you don't live with roommates, try the same idea with your Bible study friends, small group, gym buddies, or best friends. Hitting goals as a team is so rewarding and fun.

Annual Interview

This isn't something we've ever done as a family, but it's one of those things I hear about each year on social media and wish we would've done it the year before and had record of my kids when they were younger. I share this to show you that we simply can't do every great idea. Find the ones that work well for your life or family. I've seen the interview work two different ways. You have a form that is the same questions each year and filled out by the child in their own handwriting. Or you sit your kid down and video them as you ask them different questions.

Here are some examples of questions you can ask a kid in your life, but make this list your own:

- What's your name and how old are you?
- What is your favorite thing to wear?
- What is your favorite toy or item of yours?
- What is your favorite thing to do in your free time?
- What is your favorite holiday?
- What grade are you in? What is it like?
- What do you want to be when you grow up?
- Who are you friends?
- What is your favorite song?

- What is your favorite TV show?
- What is your favorite book?
- What is one thing you learned to do this year?
- What did you love most about this past year?
- What do you hope happens this next year?
- Do you have a goal for this next year?

MAKE IT *YOUR* SACRED HOLIDAY

What Are Some Ideas You've Heard of That Might Make This Holiday More Meaningful?

What Has Worked?

What Hasn't Worked?

What Do You Want to Try in the Future?

What Struggles Do You Need to Prepare For?

❑ **How to Not Be THAT Christian** *(read chapter 11)*

❑ **Realistic Expectations** *(read chapter 12)*

❑ **Conflict, Drama, and All the Feels** *(read chapter 13)*

❑ **Budgets and Generosity** *(read chapter 14)*

❑ **Schedules and Plans** *(read chapter 15)*

❑ **Grief** *(read chapter 16)*

❑ **Other:**

❑ **Other:**

❑ **Other:**

❑ **Other:**

Use the space below to list common struggles you experience for this holiday. Then take some time to list some possible solutions or things that aren't helpful. Be sure to come back here and update what worked and didn't after the holiday. Oftentimes struggles become less or more in our minds with time. This will help you handle these struggles realistically the next year.

SHARING CHALLENGE 📷 🐦

WE ALL WANT TO HEAR YOUR IDEAS! Share online what you are doing to prepare for New Year's. Be sure to use *#sacredholidays* and tag *@sacredholidays* so we can all learn from you and join in on your holy and/or set apart idea!

CHAPTER 4

VALENTINE'S DAY

To be completely transparent with you, I added and deleted this chapter from this book more times than I can count. The main reason is simply that this is just one holiday I struggle to get behind. My resistance to it has more to do with being ridiculously stubborn than even an opposition to the commercialism of this day. I hate being told what to celebrate. And I feel like every single market is wanting us to buy into this day.

I wasn't a fan of this day when I was dating in my teen and college years because of the ridiculous pressure for this day. It simply cannot live up to the expectations put out by movies, social media, and advertisements. At least not without spending an absurd amount of money or doing things you would never do on any other day of the year.

I really wasn't a fan of this season during my single years because I was just never one of those who could pretend or even be okay with being single. Don't get me wrong, I made the most of that season and I didn't spend every moment pining for what wasn't. However, if I was honest, I wanted to be in a relationship. And while I was mostly okay that I wasn't in one, this day only pointed out the obvious: still single.

Then I married the most practical man on the planet. There is not a single human on the planet who is like Chris Kiser and I love that so much about him. He isn't the guy to spend four times the amount on flowers or spend $20 on a box of four pieces of miscellaneous chocolate. He would never book a dinner at a restaurant that is overcrowded and has a "special menu" for the evening (code for "we are charging you double the price for smaller portions but dyeing something pink to make it seem like a special Valentine's Day menu"). We both say, thanks but no thanks. Basically we are the Scrooges of Valentine's Day.

I don't mean to knock it because I know so many people love this day and all its attempts to make another feel loved. You embrace this day with all of its frivolous and extravagant ways to tell others you love them. Of course you believe you should show your love to others every day, but there is something so sweet about a day set apart just to celebrate love.

Regardless of which camp we are in on Valentine's Day, I think we can find a healthy place with this day. After all, as we previously talked about, in Matthew 22:37–39, Jesus was asked what the greatest commandment was, and this is what He said: "You shall love the Lord your God with all your heart and with all your soul and with all your mind. This is the great and first commandment. And a second is like it: You shall love your neighbor as yourself."

Our God is all about love, all about it. It's the greatest commandment He had for us—love Him and love others. Pretty simple, or at least our approach to it can be. We don't have to participate in all that is expected of us this Valentine's. However, we can try our hardest to love God and love others well during this season. The world has already defined how we can best love on this day. Let's redefine our approach and love with a greater intentionality and genuine heart.

WHY DO WE CELEBRATE VALENTINE'S DAY?

The origins of this day will likely surprise you. Though no one knows for certain just how Valentine's Day began, there are a few different legends. The most commonly believed is that this day is named after a priest, St. Valentinus, who performed marriage ceremonies for Roman soldiers even though their pagan ruler forbade it. He was eventually imprisoned for this, but while imprisoned, he received countless notes from couples thanking him for choosing love over war. Another priest, also named Valentinus and imprisoned, either fell in love with his jailer's daughter or healed his jailer's daughter, and would write her letters signed, "Your Valentine." And there was yet another who preached often about the centrality of marriage and Christianity. In AD 469, one of, or all of these, St. Valentinus was given a feast, in hopes it would take the place of the pagan feasts of love and fertility with a feast of love. So, February 14 was marked on many religious calendars. It wasn't until the fourteenth century that this day was even associated with romantic love. With the rise of courtship, suitors used this day to show their love with sweets, flowers, and cards, called "valentines," to honor Saint Valentine's commitment to love.

The truth is this is one of many holidays, like Halloween, that exists today and its history serves little significance or justification for our celebration of it. All we need to know is that it is something our culture celebrates, and it's an opportunity to love others well. We are free to get behind it, as much or as little as we want. I love the freedom we get from 1 Corinthians 10:23–24, 31–33 and apply these verses to times when I'm uncertain how to approach things I'm not sure about: "'All things are lawful,' but not all things are helpful. 'All things are lawful,' but not all things build up. Let no one seek his own good, but the good of his neighbor. . . . So, whether you eat or drink, or whatever you do, do all to the glory of God. Give no offense to Jews or to Greeks or to the church of God, just as I try to please everyone in everything I do, not seeking my own advantage, but that of many, that they may be saved."

This day, if you choose to partake in it, isn't about you. This day is all about others. The beauty of this day is it shows us that it's okay, even good, to be extravagant and impractical with our love. Let's love in a way that is for "the good of [our] neighbor." I was careful to choose this verse in context. The freedom this verse mentions was given to the early church regarding whether or not to eat food in the homes of unbelievers. You see, in that day many unbelieving homes would serve meat that had been offered to pagan idols and gods. Many Christians would abstain from eating when in their homes or refuse to eat with unbelievers all together. Paul was telling them that this abstention was doing more harm than good for the sake of the gospel. He was encouraging the early church that they were free to eat whatever was before them if it didn't compromise the gospel.

I share this verse because I think sometimes, as believers, we struggle to know what to do with non-religious holidays that our neighbors celebrate in their homes and around their tables. I love how *The Message* paraphrases 1 Corinthians 10:23–24, "Looking at it one way, you could say, 'Anything goes. Because of God's immense generosity and grace, we don't have to dissect and scrutinize every action to see if it will pass muster.' But the point is not to just get by. We want to live well, but our foremost efforts should be to help others live well." Many times we can err on the side of "this is a worldly holiday, so I should pass." Or we celebrate it without our faith involved because it isn't technically a religious holiday. We need to remember that we are free to celebrate this one, as long as we invite the Lord into it, just as we invite Him to every other part of our lives.

WHY DO YOU CELEBRATE VALENTINE'S DAY?

Make Your Personal Valentine's Day
MISSION STATEMENT

Write out what you want Valentine's Day to be about (and not about).
This is where you make what was just a holiday into a Sacred Holiday—
holy and set apart. We will get to the details of how you will carry it
out, but first start with what you want this season to be about.

IDEAS FOR A MORE SACRED VALENTINE'S DAY

Don't try to do all of these ideas or try to implement all the other
ideas you've heard before. Take baby steps into each holiday. (Go
back and read chapter 1 if you need this reminder.) Pick one or
two things to try this year and do them really well. Make notes
in the white spaces of what did and didn't work, so you have a
customized resource for many years to come!

HOW TO MAKE VALENTINE'S DAY *HOLY*

Study Love (Key Word, Topical Bible Study)

If you are looking for something to do with your time with the Lord, for the month of February consider a topical study on love. Use a Bible concordance or online Bible study tool to find a list of verses on love (see the verses below to get you started). Aim to read one verse a day, but choose to really study it. Read the context, pause to find out what it means, ask the Lord what He is trying to teach about Himself, and reflect on what you need to do in response to your reading. Then pray through what you've learned—thanking God for who He is and asking Him to make you more like Him.

Verses on Love: Joshua 22:5; 1 Chronicles 16:34; Psalm 86:15; Proverbs 3:3–4; Proverbs 17:17; Song of Songs 8:6–7; Isaiah 54:10; Matthew 22:37–39; Luke 6:35; John 3:16; John 13:34–35; John 14:15; Romans 5:8; Romans 12:9–10; 1 Corinthians 13:4–7, 13; Galatians 2:20; Galatians 5:22–23; Ephesians 4:2; Ephesians 5:2; Colossians 3:14; 1 Peter 4:8; 1 John 3:16–18; 1 John 4:7–8, 18–19.

Valentine's Bags for the Homeless

Someone just recently suggested this idea in our Sacred Holidays Tribe—our private Facebook group—and I thought it was genius. Every Valentine's Day make some bags to take to the homeless and deliver them on Valentine's Day. In the bag include a meal, sweets, hygiene supplies, socks, and a Valentine's card.

If your area doesn't have a homeless ministry or shelter, there are always those in need. You could reach out to your church and ask if there is some group you could help love on in a special way if you need some direction on who to love.

Consider Those Who Might Be Lonely

During this day, whether you feel lonely yourself or not, consider others who might be feeling lonely. Take some time to identify the people in your life who might feel especially lonely this

Valentine's Day. Maybe it's a widow, a recently divorced woman, or a single girl from your neighborhood, church, or work. Maybe it's someone who is new to the area or someone whose kids have recently left home. Maybe it's some elderly people in a nursing home, sick people in a hospital, military deployed, or those incarcerated in prison. Think of some way to make them feel loved, seen, or valued. You could visit them, send them a note, invite them over, or think of a way to be thoughtful. This season can be a real hard one for a lot of people; let's make them feel extra loved today.

HOW TO MAKE VALENTINE'S DAY *SET* APART FROM THE REST OF THE YEAR

These ideas aren't always overtly spiritual, nor do they have to be. They are simply ways you can make this holiday more intentional, memorable, and distinct during the year.

Send Love Letters/Valentines to Friends and Family

Who doesn't love to get real mail? Take some time and send a handwritten note, a card, or a homemade valentine to someone(s) in your life. In your note, be sure to tell them what you love about them. If you forget to do this, there is no shame in sending text messages on Valentine's Day to those you want to be sure of your love toward them.

Leave Random Love Notes

Grab a stack of Post-its or cards, and leave random love notes in different places. This doesn't have to be romantic; in fact, don't make it romantic. Valentine's Day is a day set aside to celebrate love and to love others, not just in a romantic way. For the month of February, keep a Post-it stack in your purse, desk, car, and kitchen counter. Ask the Lord to show you when and how to encourage someone. Then write whatever you have on a note and leave it for them to find.

#GetYourFebruaryOn

My sweet friend started this hashtag years ago and it is one of my most favorite Valentine's Day traditions to do with my kids: you must wear something pink or red every day. Snap a picture and use #getyourfebruaryon when you post your picture on social media. This is a super fun and easy way to help your kids realize what season you are celebrating. It gets their mind thinking about this season. It's also a fun way to connect with a kid in your life if you aren't a mom, and plan an activity to do together that strengthens your relationship with them.

Household or Work Love-Mailboxes or Love Notes

To create a fun system to send and receive love notes to one another, use paper sacks, decorate old shoe boxes, or find some small metal mailboxes that allow for notes to be deposited throughout this holiday season. Encourage young kids to draw pictures if they can't read or write yet. If you don't want to do the mailbox thing, then have a stack of Post-its left out and leave notes for your family or coworkers sharing things you love about them.

Random Acts of Kindness

This is a great time to teach kids about loving others or prioritize it with your roommates. An easy way to do that is to have a random-acts-of-kindness challenge. Each day challenge each household member to do a specific random act of kindness. Do this for the fourteen days leading up to Valentine's Day or the entire month of February.

Teacher Love Gifts

Teachers always get a ton of gifts at Christmas time, but they get very little on Valentine's Day. One thing we started doing is not doing Christmas gifts for teachers but doing something thoughtful around Valentine's Day. Write a note yourself to a teacher in your life, or have your child write a note (or color a picture) telling them what you love about them and how grateful you are for their influence.

Send Valentines to Friends in the Mail

Think of a few loved ones you could encourage with an old-fashioned letter. Take the time to write out what you love about them. If you have kiddos in your life, pick a few friends or family members to send some homemade cards to in the mail. Let them do as much of this as possible, so it's even more meaningful. If you aren't a mom, do this craft with a kiddo in your life to help them learn what loving others in a practical way looks like. The world is constantly telling them to think only of themselves; whether you are an aunt or teacher or babysitter, don't underestimate your powerful influence in their life, setting the example of a better way!

MAKE IT *YOUR* SACRED HOLIDAY

What Are Some Ideas You've Heard of That Might Make This Holiday More Meaningful?

What Has Worked?

What Hasn't Worked?

What Do You Want to Try in the Future?

What Struggles Do You Need to Prepare For?
- ❑ **How to Not Be THAT Christian** *(read chapter 11)*
- ❑ **Realistic Expectations** *(read chapter 12)*
- ❑ **Conflict, Drama, and All the Feels** *(read chapter 13)*
- ❑ **Budgets and Generosity** *(read chapter 14)*
- ❑ **Schedules and Plans** *(read chapter 15)*
- ❑ **Grief** *(read chapter 16)*
- ❑ **Other:**

❑ **Other:**

❑ **Other:**

❑ **Other:**

Use the space below to list common struggles you experience for this holiday. Then take some time to list some possible solutions or things that aren't helpful. Be sure to come back here and update what worked and didn't after the holiday. Oftentimes struggles become less or more in our minds with time. This will help you handle these struggles realistically the next year.

SHARING CHALLENGE 📷 𝕏

WE ALL WANT TO HEAR YOUR IDEAS! Share online what you are doing to prepare for Valentine's Day. Be sure to use **#sacredholidays** and tag **@sacredholidays** so we can all learn from you and join in on your holy and/or set apart idea!

CHAPTER 5

LENT AND EASTER

I'm not sure what Easter has been about for you in the past, but I hope this becomes one of the most sacred—holy and set apart—holidays you celebrate. Your background in certain denominations will determine how familiar you are with the practice of Lent, which is the seven and a half weeks leading up to Easter. Many people believe Lent is just for Catholics. And most of what they know about Lent is that it's the time when their Catholic friends have ashes on their forehead one day and then eat a lot of fish, because that's when every fast-food chain promotes they have fish. Beyond that awareness, most people just celebrate Easter.

The truth is, for most, calling that day a celebration feels a bit like a reach. Sure, as we enter adulthood, it's become much less about the busting full baskets of Peeps and Cadbury eggs. We've exchanged that distraction for finding the perfect Easter dress and having the best Easter meal. We go to church and sing songs we fully believe, but at the end of the day it felt like it got so little attention for the magnitude of the day.

This is *the* holiday we should be celebrating! This season reminds us of the very center and story of our salvation and should be the one holiday we are all about. I am so excited for you, especially if you are new to Lent, to begin this journey of focusing on the Savior of the World who came and lived a perfect life, died on the cross for our sins, and rose to new life offering us a chance to become new creations! From death to life, this is Easter! What was once stained and darkened with sin, is now white as snow! We were once separated from God and because of Jesus' empty tomb we are given the chance to be called daughters and friends of God!

WHY DO WE CELEBRATE EASTER? WHAT IS LENT?

Easter is the celebration of the empty tomb—the resurrection Sunday that told the world that Jesus didn't just die on the cross, He rose from the dead! The cross is powerful and changes everything, but without that empty tomb the cross would mean nothing but sadness. Jesus forgives our sins, redeems our sins, and offers us a new life in Him by that empty tomb! Lent is the extension of Easter. It begins forty-six days, forty days plus six Sundays, before Easter to model the forty days Jesus fasted in the wilderness (Matt. 4:1–11). A traditional focus during Lent is a focus on prayer and repentance.

Many people practice the discipline of fasting in order to physically experience the holiday. During this time, it is very common for people to give up something that feels like a sacrifice. They might give up their favorite food or drink or give up doing something they frequently do or enjoy doing. The intent is to experience suffering ourselves, in a very modified way, to connect to the suffering of Jesus. Other common practices include Lent candles. This is similar to Advent candles, but instead of lighting a candle each week, you blow one out as you near the cross, then on Easter Sunday you light all the candles.

Like every other holiday, there isn't one right way to practice Easter and Lent. The traditions we've been passed down, along with new ones we learn, are all opportunities to connect with and glorify God. Give yourself freedom and lots of grace as you find the best practices to help focus your heart on the message of

Easter. Try different practices, one at a time, and begin celebrating that Jesus has risen, He has risen indeed!

WHY DO YOU CELEBRATE LENT AND EASTER?

Make Your Personal Easter and Lent
MISSION STATEMENT

Write out what you want Easter and Lent to be about (and not about). This is where you make what was just a holiday into a Sacred Holiday— holy and set apart. We will get to the details of how you will carry it out, but first start with what you want this season to be about.

IDEAS FOR A MORE SACRED LENT AND EASTER

Don't try to do all of these ideas or try to implement all the other ideas you've heard before. Take baby steps into each holiday. (Go back and read chapter 1 if you need this reminder.) Pick one or two things to try this year and do them really well. Make notes in the white spaces of what did and didn't work, so you have a customized resource for many years to come!

HOW TO MAKE LENT AND EASTER *HOLY*

Lent Bible Study

One of the greatest things you can do for your heart during this season is to study God's Word. Second Timothy 3:16–17 says, "All Scripture is breathed out by God and profitable for teaching, for reproof, for correction, and for training in righteousness, that the man of God may be complete, equipped for every good work." We study His Word not just because we are encouraged to "meditate on it day and night" (Josh. 1:8) or store it up in our heart (Ps. 119:11), but because this is how we hear the voice of God and know the heart of God. We don't have to guess about who He is or what matters to Him; He tells us!

During Lent I recommend doing one of two Bible study approaches: find a Lent Bible study or read through one of the Gospels. Sacred Holidays, the ministry, always offers a Lent study that is centered around the gospel story and incorporates many traditions of Lent—prompts for candle lighting, a focus on repentance, and studying the story of Jesus. However, if you want to read through a Gospel, try a forty-day reading plan (that would be six days of reading a week with a Sabbath day to focus on prayer), like this one:

Day 1: John 1:1–28

Day 2: John 1:29–51

Day 3: John 2:1–25

Day 4: John 3:1–21

Day 5: John 3:22–36

Day 6: John 4:1–42

Day 7: John 4:43–54

Day 8: John 5:1–29

Day 9: John 5:30–47

Day 10: John 6:1–21

Day 11: John 6:22–59

Day 12: John 6:60–71

Day 13: John 7:1–31

Day 14: John 7:32–53

Day 15: John 8:1–30

Day 16: John 8:31–59

Day 17: John 9:1–41

Day 18: John 10:1–21

Day 19: John 10:22–42

Day 20: John 11:1–27

Day 21: John 11:28–57

Day 22: John 12:1–26

Day 23: John 12:27–50

Day 24: John 13:1–20

Day 25: John 13:21–38

Day 26: John 14:1–14

Day 27: John 14:15–31

Day 28: John 15:1–17

Day 29: John 15:18–27

Day 30: John 16:1–15

Day 31: John 16:16–33

Day 32: John 17:1–26

Day 33: John 18:1–24

Day 34: John 18:25–40

Day 35: John 19:1–27

Day 36: John 19:28–42

Day 37: John 20:1–18

Day 38: John 20:19–30

Day 39: John 21:1–14

Day 40: John 21:15–25

Lent Candles

Using Lent candles is one of the best ways to visually experience what the heart is practicing during Lent. Like all of these practices, there isn't one specific way to set up Lent candles; you have the freedom to do this however you prefer. You will just need to have seven candles—any size, any color.

On the first day of Lent, you will light all seven candles. This first week you take in the light and think of all the ways God created light and was Himself, light. Then each week, traditionally on Sunday, you blow out one candle. As we near the cross, we visually take note of the weight of this season. That sin, darkness, has crept in and we are in desperate need of a Savior. On Good Friday you blow out the final candle and settle into the darkness. Good Friday is the day the Messiah hung on the cross for our sins, paid our punishment, and removed our separation from God. Then, the best part of all of Lent, you wake up on Easter morning and light all seven candles to celebrate that empty grave! He has risen and new life, resurrected life, is ours!

I highly recommend putting candles in a place that you sit or pass frequently. Also consider getting battery-operated candles if you have young children in your home, are afraid you might leave them burning, or just don't want to have to think about it. You might even consider having some battery-operated tea light candles at your place of work, to help you focus on the light all throughout your day. This might be a great way to share the hope of Easter with your coworkers!

Here are suggested verses you can read each time you blow out another Lent candle, and then as you light all of them on Easter morning. Again, there is not one right way to do this. These verses are just suggestions to get you started:

- Week One: Light all seven candles.
  — John 1:1–5: "In the beginning was the Word, and the Word was with God, and the Word was God. He was in the beginning with God. All things were made through him, and without him was not any thing made that was made. In him was life, and the life was the light of men. The light shines in the darkness, and the darkness has not overcome it."
- Week Two: Blow out a candle, six left lit.
  — Isaiah 42:16: "And I will lead the blind in a way that they do not know, in paths that they have not known I will guide them. I will turn the darkness before them into light, the rough places into level ground. These are the things I do, and I do not forsake them."
- Week Three: Blow out a candle, five left lit.
  — 1 Peter 2:9: "But you are a chosen race, a royal priesthood, a holy nation, a people for his own possession, that you may proclaim the excellencies of him who called you out of darkness into his marvelous light."
- Week Four: Blow out a candle, four left lit.
  — Psalm 119:105, 130: "Your word is a lamp to my feet and a light to my path. . . . The unfolding of your words gives light; it imparts understanding to the simple."
- Week Five: Blow out a candle, three left lit.
  — John 8:12: "Again Jesus spoke to them, saying, 'I am the light of the world. Whoever

follows me will not walk in darkness, but will have the light of life.'"

- Week Six: Blow out a candle, two left lit.
  — Exodus 13:21: "And the LORD went before them by day in a pillar of cloud to lead them along the way, and by night in a pillar of fire to give them light, that they might travel by day and by night."
- Week Seven: Blow out a candle, one left lit.
  — Psalm 27:1: "The LORD is my light and my salvation; whom shall I fear? The LORD is the stronghold of my life; of whom shall I be afraid?"
- Good Friday: Blow out the final candle.
  — Micah 7:8–9: "Do not gloat over me, my enemy! Though I have fallen, I will rise. Though I sit in darkness, the LORD will be my light. Because I have sinned against him, I will bear the LORD's wrath, until he pleads my case and upholds my cause. He will bring me out into the light; I will see his righteousness" (NIV).
- Easter Morning: Light all seven candles!
  — Ephesians 5:8: "For at one time you were darkness, but now you are light in the Lord. Walk as children of light."

Fasting

This is certainly an optional element to Lent, but it is one I highly recommend doing to connect with the sacrifice element of Lent.

The hardest part is choosing what you will fast from. Traditionally a Lent fast is different from a fasting-of-food-completely fast. Instead, you choose to fast from something that you really love, something that would feel like a sacrifice to go without.

It could be a certain food, an entertainment experience, or a habit that is taking up time you could be giving to the Lord.

Some people choose to fast for the entire period of Lent, while others choose to take Sundays off from their fast. There isn't a right or a wrong way to do it, so don't feel like taking a day off is cheating. You could even make it a fasting from something until you've connected with God that day. The method isn't the main thing. Just remember the intent: it should feel like a real sacrifice to the Lord.

Some verses to consider about fasting:

- *Act like yourself and keep your fast to yourself.* ("And when you fast, do not look gloomy like the hypocrites, for they disfigure their faces that their fasting may be seen by others. Truly, I say to you, they have received their reward. But when you fast, anoint your head and wash your face, that your fasting may not be seen by others but by your Father who is in secret. And your Father who sees in secret will reward you." Matt. 6:16–18)
- *Jesus fasted.* ("And after fasting forty days and forty nights, he was hungry." Matt. 4:2)
- *The early church fasted.* ("And when they had appointed elders for them in every church, with prayer and fasting they committed them to the Lord in whom they had believed." Acts 14:23)
- *Jesus said we would fast once He was no longer with the disciples on earth. It's assumed that we would practice this spiritual discipline.* ("The days will come when the bridegroom is taken away from them, and then they will fast in those days." Luke 5:35)

Go to Church

Whether you go to church every single Sunday or haven't been in years, this is a season to step into a church and try to make it home. Hebrews 10:24–25 says, "And let us consider how to stir up one another to love and good works, not neglecting to meet together, as is the habit of some, but encouraging one another, and all the more as you see the Day drawing near." When seasons get busy it can be easy to sleep in on Sundays, instead of gathering together with others to pray, worship, fellowship, and hear the Word of God spoken and taught.

During Lent there are several services that you will want to see if your church (or a church in your area) offers. Here are some examples:

- *Ash Wednesday (the first day of Lent):* Ash Wednesday isn't just for Catholics; many denominations now offer an Ash Wednesday service to kick off the first day of Lent. This service is typically focused on repentance.
- *Palm Sunday (Sunday before Easter):* This day marks the beginning of Holy Week and typically focuses on Jesus' entry into Jerusalem on a donkey as the crowds waved palm branches and shouted, "Hosanna! Hosanna in the Highest!"
- *Stations of the Cross (Typically during Holy Week):* Every church that offers this might take a different emphasis, but the focus is on praying through various elements of the betrayal and crucifixion of Jesus.
- *Good Friday (the Friday before Easter):* This is traditionally a very somber service that focuses on the death of Jesus. Remember at this point, the disciples did not know that He would rise from the dead. We step into the shoes of those who experienced that day and into the darkness they

must have felt at the death of the One who had come to save them.

- *Easter Sunday:* This is a service that is all about celebrating that He has risen!

HOW TO MAKE LENT AND EASTER *SET APART* FROM THE REST OF THE YEAR

These ideas aren't always overtly spiritual, nor do they have to be. They are simply ways you can make this holiday more intentional, memorable, and distinct during the year.

Jesus Tree

This is one of my favorite things we started doing because it helps us celebrate who Jesus is and what He has done! I take a couple of tree branches and put them in a large vase. Next to the vase, I keep a jar of small circle note cards, string, and Sharpies. I try to write something each day to celebrate who Jesus is or has been to me. Also, when others come over to our house, I invite them to share on the Jesus tree as well.

Resurrection Cards

This past year at our church, we had a station where you could write on a card what you wanted Jesus to resurrect in you during Lent and then hang it to a display. I loved this idea so much that I plan to implement this in our home. I want to be intentional about asking Jesus what things He wants to resurrect in me this year, and then put them up so I will keep bringing them before the Father in faith.

Throw a Celebration Party

You likely have some kind of meal on Easter day; why not turn that into a big celebration? Sometimes when I'm worshiping, I think about if someone who didn't know my language or customs observed me, what would they think? Would they see that I loved God? Would it be obvious? Or would the way that I worship and celebrate God be less than my excitement over big news? With this in mind, how we celebrate this day should be bigger and better than any other day we put on our calendar!

Let's go big on this day and invite others into our home. We've talked many times about gathering with others around a table as being one of the most sacred things you can do, so do it! Invite others over for a He Is Risen party! And if you have kids, have them invite their friends as well!

Messianic Passover Seder Meal

If you have the opportunity to go to one of these, say yes immediately. This meal is when Jews celebrate how the blood of a lamb saved their firstborns from certain death, and ultimately, their deliverance from Egyptian slavery. It is beautiful to see the symbolism of God's redemption then and how that correlates to His redemption today in Jesus. Facebook is another great resource to see if any friends are hosting this in their home or if any Messianic synagogues are hosting one that is open to the community. If you aren't able to find one that you can attend, but you are interested in learning more about this, you can search online about this topic and there are many guides for you to do this yourself.

Watch the Movies

We are a very visual society, and I've found that it helps me connect to the reality of Christ and the brutality of the cross by watching two movies that share the story of Jesus: *The Passion of the Christ* (2004) and *Son of God* (2014). You will want to remember that these are movies made by man and neither of them are 100 percent accurate to Scripture; nothing could be. However, it is a powerful way to visualize the times of the day, the pain of the cross, and the reality of the resurrection.

A special note for parents, guardians, and influencers of kids to read before you read the ideas below:

I know your heart is for the kids in your life to know and believe the gospel story and you want so desperately to show them as many ways as you can. Remember that raising disciples is a marathon, not a sprint. You don't need to do everything in one year. You also don't need to overdo things ever or over-spiritualize things out of fear. Show your kids the joy that Jesus brings and the hope we have in Him alone. And before you do any of these things for your kids, choose to practice them first. Be sure you don't make this holiday all about teaching them—they will learn best from watching you. As the flight attendant says, "Put your mask on first, and then take care of your kids." Do the same with your celebration of Lent. Be sure to tend to your own heart before you try to make this holiday important for little ones in your life.

Family Lent Candles

Find a way to involve your kids in using Lent candles. Let them light the candle and read the verse together about light as you do. Or maybe even let them have their own set of battery-operated candles. (Kids love being empowered and independent.) They will connect to the symbolism of this and it gives you a constant opportunity to talk to them about darkness and light, sin and salvation. If you happen to be a babysitter of someone else's kid on a weekly basis, this could be a wonderful thing you do with them each week they come to your house during the Easter season.

Focus on the Gospel Story

Let this be a season when you are intentional with sharing the salvation story with kids. During Easter I keep a basket of books by our fireplace that is filled with their storybook Bibles and other books that tell the gospel story. Read these with your kids during Lent and point out the gospel story line to them. Ask them questions and invite them to ask you questions.

Resurrection Eggs

This is not something we've done before, but I have many friends who love doing this with their kids as a way to share the story of Jesus in a creative way that has a traditional connection to Easter. You take twelve plastic eggs and place twelve prompt cards (found by searching online) inside each egg. On each card is a different part of the message of Jesus. Some open one egg a day for the twelve days leading up to Easter, while others go through them again and again throughout Lent.

MAKE IT *YOUR* SACRED HOLIDAY

What Are Some Ideas You've Heard of That Might Make This Holiday More Meaningful?

What Has Worked?

What Hasn't Worked?

What Do You Want to Try in the Future?

What Struggles Do You Need to Prepare For?

❑ **How to Not Be THAT Christian** *(read chapter 11)*

❑ **Realistic Expectations** *(read chapter 12)*

❑ **Conflict, Drama, and All the Feels** *(read chapter 13)*

❑ **Budgets and Generosity** *(read chapter 14)*

❑ **Schedules and Plans** *(read chapter 15)*

❑ **Grief** *(read chapter 16)*

❑ **Other:**

❑ **Other:**

❑ **Other:**

❑ **Other:**

Use the space below to list common struggles you experience for this holiday. Then take some time to list some possible solutions or things that aren't helpful. Be sure to come back here and update what worked and didn't after the holiday. Oftentimes struggles become less or more in our minds with time. This will help you handle these struggles realistically the next year.

SHARING CHALLENGE 📷 🐦

WE ALL WANT TO HEAR YOUR IDEAS! Share online what you are doing to prepare for Lent and Easter. Be sure to use *#sacredholidays* and tag *@sacredholidays* so we can all learn from you and join in on your holy and/or set apart idea!

CHAPTER 6

SUMMER

There is something about the ebb and flow of seasons that help us move into more figurative seasons. Whether we are operating on a school-year calendar or not, summer is definitely one of those times. I've shared how I love new beginnings and fresh starts, and summer is a great opportunity to mix things up a little or start fresh after a cold season of staying indoors (or in Texas, when we just need to make the most of the ridiculously high temps). This chapter is for all of us who are in need of a summer break (or just a break from the normal routine of life)!

WHY DO WE CELEBRATE SUMMER?

While summer isn't included on the religious calendar, it is most definitely a part of our culture and very much a season! I believe this is one that should be celebrated and participated in well past our childhood. A change in rhythm and routine. A chance to slow some things down and speed some things up. It's a mid-year start to begin new things and dream fresh dreams. It's a time for adventure, to gather with those you love, and enjoy a little warmth after winter. You maybe won't get to check out from reality for three months like you did when you were a child, but you can take your own version of summer break to refresh and enjoy life in a new way!

WHY DO YOU CELEBRATE SUMMER?

Make Your Personal Summer
MISSION STATEMENT

Write out what you want summer to be about (and not about). This is where you make what was just a holiday into a Sacred Holiday—holy and set apart. We will get to the details of how you will carry it out, but first start with what you want this season to be about.

IDEAS FOR A MORE SACRED SUMMER

Don't try to do all of these ideas or try to implement all the other ideas you've heard before. Take baby steps into each holiday. (Go back and read chapter 1 if you need this reminder.) Pick one or two things to try this year and do them really well. Make notes in the white spaces of what did and didn't work, so you have a customized resource for many years to come!

HOW TO MAKE SUMMER *HOLY*

Adjust How You Spend Time with God

I hear from women all the time that they struggle to be consistent in studying Scripture and spending time with the Lord during the summer. Some use the summer to take some time off from spending time with the Lord because schedules are so inconsistent or their church isn't doing a Bible study so they aren't sure what to do. Instead of simply finding a way to make time for God during a different season of the year, they choose to "give themselves grace" and avoid Him altogether. Know what I am about to say is because I love you so very much: this is an excuse, and it's the furthest thing from offering yourself grace.

Yes, it can be harder to spend time with the Lord during the summer because schedules feel so out of the normal and group Bible studies are much harder to come by. Not to mention it gets darker at later times of the evening, making us want to stay out longer chasing daylight and then making it harder for us to wake up. However, this just means that we need to find a new way and rhythm of connecting with the Lord during the summer.

First, take some time to look at your summer and evaluate when you should spend time with the Lord. Go ahead and block off those times on your calendar and set your alarm. These are two of the best accountabilities for staying consistent.

Second, pick what your time with the Lord will be like for the summer. You can join an online group or find a study you've been wanting to try. My favorite thing during the summer is to do a 90-day Bible reading plan. We offer free downloads for Read the Bible in 90 Days, Read the New Testament in 90 Days, and other 90-day reading plans on the Sacred Holidays website. I love reading straight Scripture in the summer because my time with the Lord feels more personal. During the year, I am often doing a group Bible study at our church or one of our holiday Bible studies. I love for my summer time with the Lord to feel more intimate, just the two of us, and free from the time lines of other commitments.

Whatever your goal or plan is for the summer, be intentional with it. If you don't hit the nail on the head every time, then yes, be quick to give yourself grace. But remember that grace isn't opting out of spending time with the Lord; true grace to you is that God gives you the space to know Him, be known by Him, and know how to better love Him and others. Enjoy that grace all summer long!

Sabbathing: Take a Vacation or Staycation (or Mental Health Day)

Growing up, one of the best parts about being a kid was that summer was one giant vacation, even if we didn't go anywhere. Take a little vacation, or staycation, this summer. Or if you would rather not travel when kids are out of school, plan a vacation this summer to take later this year. Then at the very least, maybe take a mental health day and explore your city! Resting is a good thing—something we see God the Father and the Son model for us. We don't ever want to use Scripture to justify selfish desires, but the Bible actually talks a lot about resting.

God, after creating the earth, rested on the seventh day (Gen. 2:2). We are commanded to keep the Sabbath day holy by doing all our work for six days and then doing absolutely no work on the seventh (Exod. 20:8–9). Our culture is pretty horrible about this, and Sabbath is just not something we practice. However, it was one of the Ten Commandments, so this is something the Lord saw as valuable for His chosen people. Then we observe Jesus all throughout the Gospels, retreating by Himself. Obviously, Sabbath and vacation aren't exactly the same thing, but the principle is the same—rest from work for a time.

HOW TO MAKE SUMMER *SET APART* FROM THE REST OF THE YEAR

These ideas aren't always overtly spiritual, nor do they have to be. They are simply ways you can make this holiday more intentional, memorable, and distinct during the year.

Summer Bucket List

Bucket lists are something you either love or hate. Let me free you from it if they in any way overwhelm you. I happen to love them because they help me make the most of the season. I love planning and setting goals, so I function really well with a bucket list. However, if you don't love this, maybe instead of a bucket list you can pick one to five things you want to make sure you do this summer. Or just keep your summer mission statement, that you wrote above, front and center so you are checking your days against that.

If you do want to do a bucket list, obviously you can find hundreds of ideas online, but here's a list of ideas we shared with our Sacred Holidays tribe last summer broken into categories:

TASTE

❑ Snow cones ❑ Watermelon ❑ Root Beer Floats ❑ Grill Out ❑ S'mores ❑ Create a New Recipe ❑ Farmer's Market ❑ Make Homemade Ice Cream ❑ Food Truck Dinner ❑ Picnic at the Park ❑ Breakfast for Dinner ❑ Try a New Patio Restaurant ❑ Homemade Pizza ❑ Bake Something from Scratch ❑ Pick Fruit ❑ Make Banana Splits ❑ Progressive Dinner ❑ Go Vegan for the Day ❑ Invite Your Neighbors Over for a Meal ❑ Choose an Ethnic Restaurant

MOVE IT

❑ Driving Range ❑ Dance in the Rain ❑ Kayak ❑ Frisbee Golf ❑ Learn a New Dance ❑ Play Twister ❑ Play Catch ❑ Wash Your Car ❑ Outdoor Yoga Class ❑ Batting Cages ❑ Shoot Hoops ❑ Do a Fun Run ❑ Roller-Skate ❑ Try

CrossFit or a Gym Class ❑ Set a New Goal (+ Reach It!) ❑ Do 100 Crunches ❑ Run One Mile ❑ Go for a Bike Ride

THE OUTDOORS

❑ Go to the Beach ❑ Water Balloon Fight ❑ Swim in a Pool ❑ Collect Sea Shells ❑ Wake Up to Watch the Sunrise ❑ Shoot Off Fireworks ❑ Fish ❑ Hike ❑ Flea Market ❑ Create an Herb Garden ❑ Carve Name in Tree ❑ Swing at the Playground ❑ Fly a Kite ❑ Night Swim ❑ Skip Rocks ❑ Pick Wild Flowers ❑ Make a Campfire ❑ Visit Botanical Garden or Arboretum ❑ Catch Fireflies ❑ Lounge in a Hammock ❑ Enjoy a Summer Breeze

STAY IN

❑ Read a Book ❑ Board Games ❑ DIY Spa Day ❑ Sew Something ❑ Use Watercolors ❑ PJ + Movies Day ❑ Start to Learn a New Language ❑ Play Cards ❑ Bowl ❑ Redecorate a Room ❑ Read an eBook ❑ Do Something You've Pinned ❑ Take a Nap ❑ Re-create a Famous Painting ❑ Listen to a New Podcast ❑ Update Your Résumé ❑ Change Your Profile Picture ❑ Make a Spotify Playlist ❑ Try New Makeup Looks ❑ Write a Poem

ADVENTURE

❑ Geocaching ❑ Ride a Ferris Wheel ❑ Last-Minute Road Trip ❑ Go Camping (in a Tent) ❑ Tube a River ❑ Visit a State Park ❑ Learn a New Sport ❑ Take a Cooking Class ❑ Try to Make a World Record ❑ Make + Bury a Time Capsule ❑ Overcome a Fear ❑ Ride a Rollercoaster ❑ Explore a City Nearby ❑ Be a Tourist in Your City ❑ Research Local Free Events + Go to One ❑ Make a Dream Board ❑ See a Band Play Live ❑ Go Play Bingo

ENTERTAINMENT

❏ Drive-In Movie ❏ Baseball Game ❏ Art Museum
❏ Karaoke ❏ Painting Class ❏ Make a Baby Smile
❏ Watermelon Seed Spitting Contest ❏ Host Christmas in
July Party ❏ Watch a Comedian ❏ Go to a Play

LOVE OTHERS

❏ Take Treats to Your Firemen ❏ Send a Card in the Mail
❏ Make a New Friend ❏ Pay for the Meal of the Car in Line
Behind You ❏ Sponsor a Child through Compassion ❏ Visit a
Retirement Center ❏ No Screen Time Day ❏ Donate Unused
Clothes ❏ Skype with an Old Friend ❏ Choose to Forgive
❏ Give a Compliment ❏ Leave a Big Tip ❏ Encourage an
Orphan Worker/Parent ❏ Feed Someone Who Is Hungry
❏ Smile + Say Hi More

Remember, these are just suggestions to get you started. Spend some time brainstorming about what would make for a fun, refreshing, and purposeful summer for you. Each year we release an updated, free "Summer Bucket List for Women" download. This is not meant to stress you out or cause you to feel overwhelmed. You will likely not do everything on this list, or whatever list you create. The point is that you would have a more intentional summer because you are more focused for it to be a certain way. To make this even more fun, ask some girlfriends to join you!

Summer Bucket List for the Kiddos in Your Life

This is one of our favorite summer traditions. These lists can get a little crazy, so make a list that sounds fun for you and the kiddos in your life! No matter what part you play in a child's life, they will never forget these lasting memories with you. Below is a list of ideas we shared with our Sacred Holidays tribe last summer broken into categories. (Each year we release an updated, free "Summer Bucket List for Kids" download.)

FOOD

❑ Fruit Picking ❑ Make Popsicles ❑ Homemade Pizza ❑ Watermelon ❑ Root Beer Floats ❑ S'mores ❑ Lemonade Stand ❑ Kids Make a Meal ❑ Homemade Ice Cream ❑ Food Truck ❑ Breakfast for Dinner ❑ Farmer's Market ❑ Snow Cones ❑ Some Place New

GET OUT

❑ Identify Cloud Shapes ❑ Fry an Egg on the Sidewalk ❑ Backyard Campout ❑ Sidewalk Chalk ❑ Catch Fireflies ❑ Watch Fireworks Show ❑ Go to the Zoo ❑ Visit a Farm ❑ Fly a Kite ❑ Feed Ducks ❑ Scavenger Hunt ❑ Ride a Carousel ❑ Climb a Tree ❑ Swing ❑ Ride a Train or Trolley

FOR THE RAINY DAYS

❑ $1 Movie ❑ Library ❑ Board Game ❑ No Screen Time for a Day ❑ Make a Puppet Show ❑ Quiet Game ❑ Play 20 Questions ❑ Sheet Fort ❑ Rock, Paper, Scissors ❑ Homemade Playdough ❑ New Lego Kit ❑ PJ + Movies Day ❑ Write a Song ❑ Skype with a Friend ❑ Draw a Self-Portrait ❑ Paper Airplane ❑ Cereal Necklace ❑ Pillow Fight

WET OR MESSY

❑ Sand Castle ❑ Water Balloon Fight ❑ Bubbles ❑ Splash in Rain Puddles ❑ Pool ❑ Silly String Fight ❑ Run through the Sprinklers ❑ Make Tie-Dye Shirts ❑ Collect Sea Shells ❑ Slip-n-Slide ❑ Water Gun Fight ❑ Paint Pottery ❑ Wash the Car ❑ Splash Pad ❑ Write in Shaving Cream ❑ Night Swim or Bath Time with Glow Sticks

GET ENERGY OUT

❑ Putt-Putt Golf ❑ Nature Walk ❑ Bowling ❑ Hopscotch ❑ Simon Says ❑ Family Fun Run ❑ Freeze Tag ❑ Hula Hoop Contest ❑ Fishing ❑ Trampoline ❑ Hide-n-Seek ❑ Roll Down a Hill ❑ Red Light, Green Light ❑ Go to a New Playground

LEARN NEW THINGS

❑ Home Depot Kids Workshops ❑ 10 Words in Spanish ❑ Magic Trick ❑ Conquer a Fear ❑ Read Books (pick a number) ❑ Library Story Time ❑ Recreate Famous Art Work ❑ Make Family Tree and Share Stories ❑ Try a New Sport ❑ Research a Country ❑ Interview Someone

GO SOMEWHERE

❑ Beach ❑ Fourth of July Parade ❑ Baseball Game ❑ Slumber Party ❑ Waterpark ❑ State Park ❑ Explore City Nearby ❑ Research Free Community Events ❑ State Capitol

LOVE OTHERS

❑ Collect Items for Pregnancy Center ❑ Do Yard Work for a Neighbor ❑ Encourage Someone Who Helps Orphans ❑ Visit a Nursing Home ❑ Bake Treats for Doctors Office or Kids Ministry Team at Church ❑ Send Cards to Extended Family ❑ Include Someone ❑ Give a Compliment ❑ Volunteer at a Nonprofit ❑ Write Your Mayor, Senator + President ❑ Donate Clothes + Toys ❑ Do Extra Chores

Hit Refresh on New Year's Goals (Or Make a New Goal!)

Summer marks exactly halfway through the calendar year! Can you believe it? This is a great time to sit down and reflect on how you are doing for the goals you set at the beginning of the year. It is always a great time to choose a smaller goal, something you want to accomplish that summer.

Whether you are hitting refresh on your new year goals or setting a new goal for the summer, invite others into your process. Have a goal-setting night with friends and then think of ways you can check in on your goals throughout the summer. Think of ways you can best support and encourage one another as you go after your goals.

Take a Break from Screen Time

Take advantage of the fact that your favorite shows aren't releasing new episodes for the summer. And, for the love, let's put our phones down. We are becoming a culture that is better at observing what others are posting about their lives than living our own. I feel like each week I read a new study that shares about the devastating effects of all of our screen time. For women, the worst has to be the shaming we inflict on ourselves: *Why isn't our life more like hers? Why can't we look that way? Our lives are so lame compared to others!* Ladies, these are lies! I find that I'm so much happier when I limit how often I'm on my phone. There is so much good to our phones and what we can do with them. We are better connected to one another than ever before. It's beautiful. But all the scrolling can also be a little excessive sometimes.

So this summer, choose to put the phone down more. Set some healthier boundaries on it like keeping the phone on a counter instead of by your side, only check social media once or twice a day, and unfollow accounts that bring more shame than joy.

Summer Countdown and Celebration

The month before school ends, I typically start a countdown chain to summer. This is a fun way to build excitement for my girls that summer, our favorite season, is coming! Even though I am barely hanging on by the end of the year when it comes to making lunches and remembering to sign folders, I try to make the last week of school super fun, and then make the last day of school and first day of summer feel like a party. I do a banner, streamers, and balloons. I bought a banner the first year, and then spend all of five dollars on the streamers and balloons. The effort is totally worth it for my girls—they love it!

Find what would feel like a celebration for you! If you don't live with the kids in your life, think outside of the box. Send them a fun little summer care package in the mail (everyone loves real mail) or send a video message to celebrate the start of summer.

Go Over or Make Family Rules

Whether you have kids with you for an hour, a week, or longer stretches, I highly recommend sitting down and coming up with your summer rules, or just reinforcing your regular family rules.

We did this for the first time last summer because after week one of summer break, my kiddos were totally taking advantage of my desire for it to be a fun summer. They were out of control and I was not happy. So we sat down and listed our rules on the chalkboard in our kitchen: Be kind, be respectful, use your manners, don't fuss or fight, be grateful, love others well, and have fun! We all agreed on the rules and spent some time going over what they meant. Then, most mornings or before we would go somewhere, we would go over the rules.

As you talk about the rules, also talk about what the consequences will be if the rules aren't followed. The more consistent you are with your consequences, the better your kiddos will stick with the rules. Also, consider rewards. If your kids had exceptional attitudes or you notice them trying really hard in a certain situation, take time to praise them or give them a special reward.

Reading and Book Clubs

Every teacher friend has told me that summer brain is a real thing (for both kids and adults!) and that kids typically take a while to get back into the groove of school. The best recommendation they have is to stay on top of reading over the summer. Many schools have reading trackers or lists to help guide you or a kid in your life through this. One of the best things about reading is it gives you or a child some quiet time built into your day. The library is one of our favorite places to go during the summer. We love all the options they have—plus it's free!

Consider hosting a book club for some of your friends or for the kids in your life. If your kids are younger, parents could take turns having story time at their house. If your kids are older, they could all read the chapter book and have a discussion time. Kids could also have a book-trading club. So each time they meet, they trade books. If you do this with friends your own age, the same can apply. The house-host can change, as well as responsibilities for refreshments.

Let Them (or Yourself) Get Bored

Sometimes we can fill up the summers so full with activities, that we forget to just let ourselves be, or for the kids in our lives, to just let them be kids. Boredom isn't a bad thing. Our culture has become so entertainment- and instant-gratification-centered that we don't know what to do with empty space. If your kids aren't sure what to do with their boredom, maybe help them come up with a list of ten things they can do when they are bored. They might find this list boring, but that's not your problem (ha!). If you are the one struggling with boredom, make your own list. Give yourself time to journal, walk, think, listen to music, draw, or create something. Boredom is actually where creativity is at its highest!

Back to School

As summer comes to a close, find ways to be a support to all of those who are going back to school. Here are some suggestions:

- Send notes of encouragement to teacher friends.
- Give gift cards to teachers (setting up rooms is an out-of-pocket expense for teachers!).
- Adopt your local public school: gather some neighbors or your church and reach out to a local public school and see how you can support them. If it's a lower-income school, they might need help getting school supplies. Or maybe you could

volunteer to throw some teacher-appreciation events. Just because you don't have kids at the school you are zoned to doesn't mean you can't be involved in loving your (school) neighbors!

- Encourage your mom friends. Many will be thrilled that their kids are going to school, and just as many will be super sad to have them back in school.

Make going back to school for the kids in your life just as fun of an experience as summer starting. Here are some ways you can do that:

- Make a back-to-school countdown chain. This will be helpful for them and you to prepare for the summer ending and the school days, with their routines, coming back.
- Get back-to-school ready: pull out the backpacks and lunch boxes, figure out back-to-school out-fits, and whatever else helps your kids get ready!
- Order or go get all your back-to-school supplies. I know most schools have you order the supplies online now, but it's still fun for kids to go pick out a few special supplies. My girls get to go and pick out three supplies for their backpacks or home.
- Have them make their teacher a card or pick out a small gift.

Back-to-School Grade or Class Party

To help us get to know a new area after moving, I offered to host a playdate at our house for the incoming kindergartners in my daughter's class. It ended up being such a great way to meet other kids, and two of the girls who came to that are still some of her best friends. It was also so great for me to have a group of moms that I could reach out to. Since then, we've hosted a few class gatherings at our house as a way to get to know the kids in my daughter's classes.

MAKE IT *YOUR* SACRED HOLIDAY

What Are Some Ideas You've Heard of That Might Make This Holiday More Meaningful?

What Has Worked?

What Hasn't Worked?

What Do You Want to Try in the Future?

What Struggles Do You Need to Prepare For?

❏ **How to Not Be THAT Christian** *(read chapter 11)*

❏ **Realistic Expectations** *(read chapter 12)*

❏ **Conflict, Drama, and All the Feels** *(read chapter 13)*

❏ **Budgets and Generosity** *(read chapter 14)*

❏ **Schedules and Plans** *(read chapter 15)*

❏ **Grief** *(read chapter 16)*

❏ **Other:**

❏ **Other:**

❏ **Other:**

❏ **Other:**

Use the space below to list common struggles you experience for this holiday. Then take some time to list some possible solutions or things that aren't helpful. Be sure to come back here and update what worked and didn't after the holiday. Oftentimes struggles become less or more in our minds with time. This will help you handle these struggles realistically the next year.

SHARING CHALLENGE

WE ALL WANT TO HEAR YOUR IDEAS! Share online what you are doing to prepare for summer. Be sure to use *#sacredholidays* and tag @ *sacredholidays* so we can all learn from you and join in on your holy and/ or set apart idea!

CHAPTER 7

HALLOWEEN

I know there will be some that pick up this book and will be offended that I included a holiday like Halloween in a book about sacred holidays. At Sacred Holidays, the ministry, we always lose a few followers when we share about the awesomeness that can be Halloween. After all, isn't Halloween Satan's holiday? I hope to enlighten you on some (mis)perceptions about that idea throughout this chapter.

If you are fearful of the pagan connections tied to this holiday, let me ask you to just give this chapter a chance. You don't have to agree with me. My hope is only that you hear another approach to this day. Then you take all of this to your Father and process it through with Him. I don't believe there is a right way to approach this day. If at the end of this chapter, you still aren't comfortable with it, that is totally fine. The Lord knows your heart, just as He knows mine, and there is much grace and love from Him.

Before we talk about why we celebrate Halloween and ways we can celebrate it in a more sacred—holy and set apart—way, I wanted to share a story with you that I hope makes you laugh a little and helps you understand why I love this day so very much.

Some people grow up with moms who make their homes into Christmas villages. Back in the day, when I was a kid, Christmas sweaters were something the super Christmas moms actually wore and not as a joke. My mom wasn't exactly like that. My mom's jam was Halloween. Beginning October 1, she would begin only talking in her witch voice, complete with a believable cackle. We would string cobwebs in the windows and wait for the day with as much anticipation as kids at Christmas. There was nothing pagan or anything like that rooted in our obsession with the day. Like most people who get into this day, it was just a day about make-believe and lots of candy, and for those reasons it was one of my most favorite days of the year. This particular Halloween I was eight and I only wanted to be one thing that year—the lead character from my very favorite movie that had released that year. Many good movies released in 1990 like *Teenage Mutant Ninja Turtles*, *Home Alone*, *Kindergarten Cop*, *3 Men and a Little Lady*, *Problem Child*, and *Captain America*. Like any good '90s child, I could've dressed as my favorite turtle that year, but no, that wasn't my favorite movie. Neither were any of those others. My favorite movie was *Pretty Woman*. Yes, for some reason I was allowed to watch that movie and that year all I wanted to be was Vivian. But not Vivian post Rodeo Drive, but Vivian at the beginning of the movie. And somehow, that same mom who began cackling on October 1 also thought it was okay for me to be Vivian for Halloween. So I borrowed her knee-high boots, that came up to my thighs and rolled up my shortest skirt, flipped my shirt into that loopy thing we used to do back in those days to make our shirts crop tops, crimped my hair because it was the '90s, and put on my mom's brightest lipstick. I looked every bit of the eight-year-old version of Vivian. Please, dear friend, tell me you are laughing at this scene.

This night was the night I still remember; and now that I'm a believer, I'll never forget the love I experienced. That year we weren't able to go trick-or-treating because it was storming so bad. So my mom took us to the mall because the stores used to hand out candy.

But it was pretty boring. So we piled back into our little Plymouth Horizon in search of some kid-friendly Halloween fun. Driving around our neighborhood, we saw in bright lights: "Rain or Shine! Fall Festival. Lots of Candy!" We screeched into the parking lot and ran into that church's gym ready to redeem this dreary day. And it was wonderful—games everywhere and tons of candy. But the best part of all was at every single booth those sweet Baptist volunteers would lean down and ask me, "And who are you, sweetie?" I would straighten up proudly and say with the confidence of Vivian herself, "I am Pretty Woman!" The look—a mix of shock and sweetness. I can see it now and it just makes me laugh so very hard. They loved me well. A girl, her brother, and a single mom who didn't go to church were loved that day, dressed as a hooker and all!

This is why I love Halloween and love for Christians to open their doors on this day: it is the one day of the year your neighbors knock on your door! Let's be there to open it! One of our greatest commandments is to love our neighbors (Mark 12:30–31). Obviously, you can still love your neighbors and not participate in Halloween. But what other day of the year do your neighbors knock on your door and walk around your street in groups? Let's be there to greet them. Let's love them right where they are, even if they have costumes we aren't comfortable with. This holiday is whatever you choose to make it. The day is already set aside; it's up to us to make it sacred—holy and set apart.

WHY DO WE CELEBRATE HALLOWEEN?

If you look into the history of Halloween, it's origin has actually been disputed for quite some time. Believe it or not, Halloween has been historically celebrated on various liturgical calendars over the course of Christian history as a day to either remember the dead, or in the Catholic tradition, to pray for souls thought to be in purgatory. I know, still morbid. The belief that this holiday is a satanic one comes from the widely held belief that Halloween came out of the Celtic harvest festivals, and those festivals may, or may not, have some pagan roots. Did you know that the word

Halloween actually means "holy evening" and is of Christian origin? I'm not trying to baptize this day into become an overtly Christian holiday. I'm just trying to help break a stereotype that was created and has kept many, out of fear of being supporters of anything related to Satan, from being a part of Halloween.

Today, the reason people celebrate Halloween has very little to do with its Christian or Celtic origins. Now it is simply a day of dressing up and eating a ridiculous amount of candy. Yes, some still like to get into the scary and spooky of the day, but it is very rarely done in a demonic way.

For Christians, I think it's an important time for us to love others well. As I've already shared, it's the one day of the year that our neighbors knock on our doors. On top of that, the Christian community has, unintentionally, done a lot of damage making unbelievers feel judged during this time of year with their "shame for celebrating a demonic holiday" comments and attitudes. Let's redeem some of the fear and hate that has been wrongly spread. This holiday, like so many others, is simply whatever you choose to make it.

I hear people say often that we are called to be "in the world but not of the world" and this phrase confuses me so much. It's not a verse in the Bible; did you know that? We quote it so much in the church that many of us believe it must be somewhere. It originates from Jesus' prayer in John 17. In this prayer Jesus proclaims that He came to them (the disciples) and that He was not of the world, and that His disciples weren't of the world either (vv. 14 and 16). Then verse 18 says, "As you sent me into the world, so I have sent them into the world." Hence the saying: in the world, not of the world. However, we've somehow interpreted this to mean that we are in this world, but we aren't to have anything to do with it. If we draw this conclusion, then we've missed verse 15, which states, "I do not ask that you take them out of the world, but that you keep them from the evil one." Jesus' desire wasn't our removal from the world or those in it. He didn't commission us to be isolated in our safe Christian bubbles. He sent us into the world, and He prayed for our protection from the evil one. We wouldn't need a prayer of protection if we weren't stepping into places where evil was. Let's not step out of this world; it wasn't Jesus' heart.

I commission you into this next section with Matthew 5:14–16, "You are the light of the world. A city set on a hill cannot be hidden. Nor do people light a lamp and put it under a basket, but on a stand, and it gives light to all in the house. In the same way, let your light shine before others, so that they may see your good works and give glory to your Father who is in heaven." My hope for every single woman reading this book is that you would see this day, that has so much darkness associated with it, and you would use it to shine brightly for the name of Jesus. My prayer for you is that Jesus would use the light you shine to bring great glory to Him and draw many to Him. They notice your good works. May faith come from them in Jesus' name!

WHY DO YOU CELEBRATE HALLOWEEN?

Make Your Personal Halloween
MISSION STATEMENT

Write out what you want Halloween to be about (and not about). This is where you make what was just a holiday into a Sacred Holiday—holy and set apart. We will get to the details of how you will carry it out, but first start with what you want this season to be about.

IDEAS FOR A MORE SACRED HALLOWEEN

Don't try to do all of these ideas or try to implement all the other ideas you've heard before. Take baby steps into each holiday. (Go back and read chapter 1 if you need this reminder.) Pick one or two things to try this year and do them really well. Make notes in the white spaces of what did and didn't work, so you have a customized resource for many years to come!

HOW TO MAKE HALLOWEEN *HOLY*

Pray Over Your Street

Knowing your neighbors will be out and about and you will have the chance to love on them soon, take a few walks around your neighborhood leading up to Halloween. Use that time to pray over each home you pass and the people who live there. Ask the Lord to increase your heart and love for those who live on your street. Ask for His creativity in loving them and showing that love and light to them on Halloween and all year long.

Be Home with the Lights On and Door Open

If you've never done anything for Halloween, and the makes you uncomfortable, start here with just this one idea home, turn your light on, and hand out treats for the kids time you open the door, ask the Lord to let you be a light face of love. Ooh and aah over every kid who comes to y Thank the Lord that your neighbors are knocking on and ask Him to give you more opportunities and ways neighbors well that next year.

One dilemma many are faced with this da church will host a Fall Festival on Halloween, and if they should invite neighbors to that and vol they should stay home. I completely understan my first answer is that you simply pray abou decision you think is best. If you still aren't sure what to do, I'll say it again: this is the one night a year your neighbors knock on your door. I love Fall Festivals. Obviously, I still remember the one I went to that rainy Halloween in the '90s. I even used to coordinate the Fall Festival when I was on staff at a megachurch in Houston. There is so much good about Fall Festivals. With that said, if you don't need to be there, stay home. I would also encourage you to talk to your church about considering to host their Fall Festival on a day that isn't Halloween. That way it can be an outreach for the community, but one that doesn't take the body of Christ off the streets in their neighborhoods on Halloween. If you do decide to go to a Fall Festival instead, which is totally fine, then leave your light on and have a bucket of candy on your porch with a sign that says to take a couple of pieces.

HOW TO MAKE HALLOWEEN *SET APART* FROM THE REST OF THE YEAR

These ideas aren't always overtly spiritual, nor do they have to be. They are simply ways you can make this holiday more intentional, memorable, and distinct during the year.

Be the Best House on the Block (or Apartment in the Building)

If you want to go one step further than being home with the lights on, go all out and be the very best house on the block or apartment in the building! Maybe not the best; you don't need to be the Clark Griswold of Halloween. It's not about a competition with your neighbors. I'm simply encouraging you to utilize your creativity, or the endless supply of ideas on the Internet, to be the house people *want* to drop by. A few things to consider:

- Give away good treats—stand out as the house to hit up twice! Maybe you have a special treat for older kids. I know some houses that give full-size candy bars to teenagers and adults. One house

I went to this year handed out a special, home-made treat just for the adults. It was so thoughtful! I think of their generosity every single time I pass their house. Regardless, pick candy or treats that you would want to have. If you aren't sure, ask kids what they love getting and then pick those out.

- Set up a hangout in your front yard (if you have a yard and driveway). We started doing this about five years ago and it has changed our Halloweens. We pull out our patio furniture and fire pit to the drive and blast music and invite people to hang out.
- Rent an inflatable. We went in with some friends to do this one year and it was a huge hit! If you want kids to come back and adults to hang out, then doing something like this is a great way to get people to stay and hang out.
- Consider those with food allergies and have an option for them. Most parents whose kids have food allergies typically have a back-up plan in place for this day, but you will earn a Food Allergy Mama's love forever if you have a teal pumpkin (a sign that your treats are all allergy friendly).
- Instead of having food-based treats, hit up the dollar store and have a bunch of fun toys to choose from. I've found that kids LOVE all things that glow, and parents love their kids having these while trick-or-treating too!
- Serve something that might encourage people to hang around. This past year we were going to have a s'mores station (the torrential downpour that night cancelled those plans). Grill hotdogs

or have a hot chocolate station. Whatever sounds fun for you!

Obviously, many of the ideas cost money. I'm not encouraging you to go into debt over Halloween, but as you begin taking baby steps into making holidays sacred, consider Halloween when you are setting your budget. Dream about the things you'd like to do in the future and set aside money to make that happen.

Host a Gathering for Neighbors

Some families on a cul-de-sac down the street from us host a Halloween gathering from 5–6 p.m. every Halloween. They provide pizza for everyone, and a retired man gives hayrides to all the kids around the neighborhood. At 6 p.m. the kids are all released to go trick-or-treating. It's a beautiful way to meet neighbors who haven't come out all year long or have recently moved. Think of what might work for you.

If you live in an apartment, talk to your office staff to see if they'd be interested in hosting a party. Most apartments have a budget for events. This could be a great way to not only reach out to your neighbors but build a good relationship with the staff at your complex or the management for your building.

Organize Something Fun for Your Coworkers

Don't keep the fun limited to just loving your neighbors. Make it a fun day at work (if your boss allows or you are the boss). Most adults love to have fun on this day too. Gather a few coworkers and plan a fun day using some of the ideas in this chapter or coming up with some new ideas! Even if your work doesn't do something officially that day, prepare a little treat for each of your coworkers that day and deliver it to them that morning.

Pumpkin Carving

This is something you can do with friends, family, neighbors, coworkers—whomever! As we talk about often in this book, there is something very sacred about gathering with others. Let this night be a night with lots of laughter that you were able to gift to other people. This doesn't have to cost anything except the cost of your pumpkin and carving tools. If you invite others into it, have them bring their own pumpkin and tools. You could turn it into an annual contest. The point of this is to have lots of fun and get a little slimy in the process!

Get into It by Dressing Up

Embrace this day for all its silliness. I know you are a grown-up, and you think you should play it cool now. Don't do that; it's so much more fun to dress up. I can also guarantee it that you will have more neighbors engage with you if you embrace wearing a costume. You don't have to go full-out, although that's awesome; you can wear a fun wig, hat, or shirt. Just do something that is a little more than just wearing a black shirt with jeans.

If You Still Don't Like It, Give Grace to Those Who Do

I know there were some of you who started this chapter unsure or maybe even entirely against Halloween, and maybe your feelings still haven't changed about this day. First, let me thank you for being open and giving Halloween a chance. Second, you are fully entitled to feel how you do about this day. The only thing I would encourage you is to give grace to those who feel differently. There are some, and I'm not saying this has been you, who feel like it's their mission to make sure everyone knows it's Satan's holiday. So anytime other Christians post about this day, they feel it is their mission to proclaim that it is demonic and to speak shame over the person celebrating the day. Let's not be those people. Let's respect and love one another well even when we disagree.

Boo-ing Friends and Neighbors

One of my favorite things my girls get to do at Halloween is to "Boo" their friends. How it works is you make a little bucket full of goodies and leave it on a friend or neighbor's porch with a sign that says, "You've been boo-ed!" My girls love getting to go pick out goodies and fill the buckets. This doesn't need to be a budget buster; kids just love the surprise element of it, so hit up the dollar store! You can find printables and ideas for this online.

Pumpkin Painting Party

One of our favorite traditions is to gather our friends and their kiddos together to paint little pumpkins. Everyone has their kids bring a little pumpkin, a few paint brushes, and a pumpkin food item for an All Things Pumpkin picnic and painting party. I just use regular washable (because us mamas need all things to be washable) art paint, squirt a few colors on a plate, and the kids get in a giant circle and paint. We typically do this to kick off the month of October. What's great about painted pumpkins is they don't go bad, at least not quickly. So your kid's beautiful creation will last all the way to Halloween.

Go to a Farm or Pumpkin Patch

This is one of our favorite traditions to do each year! Research if you have a farm near your home that you could visit. A lot of farms will have corn mazes, pumpkin patches, hayrides, and other fall festivities. This is a fun way to kick off the fall season as a family or a group of friends. If you don't have a farm nearby, see if any businesses or churches in your area have pumpkin patches. There is something so magical for kids to see so many pumpkins, plus it allows you to get a super cute pic of your little pumpkin! There's also value in children seeing people who aren't their parents enjoying a holiday like this in clean ways, so even if you aren't a parent, don't underestimate your example in front of children this time of year.

MAKE IT *YOUR* SACRED HOLIDAY

What Are Some Ideas You've Heard of That Might Make This Holiday More Meaningful?

What Has Worked?

What Hasn't Worked?

What Do You Want to Try in the Future?

What Struggles Do You Need to Prepare For?

❑ **How to Not Be THAT Christian** *(read chapter 11)*

❑ **Realistic Expectations** *(read chapter 12)*

❑ **Conflict, Drama, and All the Feels** *(read chapter 13)*

❑ **Budgets and Generosity** *(read chapter 14)*

❑ **Schedules and Plans** *(read chapter 15)*

❑ **Grief** *(read chapter 16)*

❑ **Other:**

❑ **Other:**

❑ **Other:**

❑ **Other:**

Use the space below to list common struggles you experience for this holiday. Then take some time to list some possible solutions or things that aren't helpful. Be sure to come back here and update what worked and didn't after the holiday. Oftentimes struggles become less or more in our minds with time. This will help you handle these struggles realistically the next year.

SHARING CHALLENGE 📷 🐦

WE ALL WANT TO HEAR YOUR IDEAS! Share online what you are doing to prepare for Halloween. Be sure to use *#sacredholidays* and tag *@sacredholidays* so we can all learn from you and join in on your holy and/or set apart idea!

CHAPTER 8

THANKSGIVING

Finally comes the season of all things pumpkin. I don't know about you, but I go a little pumpkin crazy. I get all the pumpkins. I burn pumpkin candles and buy pumpkin soap. When I go to the grocery store I buy every single pumpkin-flavored thing without shame or consideration of the budget. (Apologies to all of you who don't love all things pumpkin; this must be a super annoying season for you.) With all things pumpkin, this is also the season of all things gratitude. Across our country, our specific expressions of this holiday differ but our hearts are all very much aligned: we want to give thanks! However, in the whirlwind of the holidays picking up speed, we can't forget to do just that.

WHY DO WE CELEBRATE THANKSGIVING?

Traditionally, Thanksgiving (or "day of thanksgiving") was set up to celebrate a harvest of God's favor, protection, and blessing. George Washington first declared it a national holiday in November 1789, more than one hundred years from the first documented one in Plymouth in 1621 (though rumor has it that some colonies boasted a day of thanks before even that date!). As very few of us still celebrate an actual harvest, it is now a cultural celebration of giving thanks for all we have received this past year.

It's a season to count our blessings and celebrate with gratitude with others.

WHY DO YOU CELEBRATE THANKSGIVING?

Make Your Personal Thanksgiving
MISSION STATEMENT

Write out what you want Thanksgiving to be about (and not about). This is where you make what was just a holiday into a Sacred Holiday— holy and set apart. We will get to the details of how you will carry it out, but first start with what you want this season to be about.

IDEAS FOR A MORE SACRED THANKSGIVING

Don't try to do all of these ideas or try to implement all the other ideas you've heard before. Take baby steps into each holiday. (Go back and read chapter 1 if you need this reminder.) Pick one or two things to try this year and do them really well. Make notes in the white spaces of what did and didn't work, so you have a customized resource for many years to come!

HOW TO MAKE THANKSGIVING *HOLY*

30 Days of Gratitude

In the crazy whirlwind of life, we can forget to be intentional about being grateful to God. I find it really helpful to do a 30 Days of Gratitude Challenge. Take time to journal about these with the Lord, and then share about it on social media if you'd like. I find sharing it on social media is good accountability to keep with it, and it is also a beautiful way to give glory to God on what He has done in your life.

Here is a 30 Day #SacredHolidays Gratitude Prompt Plan for your time with the Lord:

Nov 1: Family or Family Member

Nov 2: Your City

Nov 3: Your Home

Nov 4: Your Job or Daily Tasks

Nov 5: BFF/Spouse/Significant Other

Nov 6: Feelings

Nov 7: The Weather

Nov 8: A Challenge You've Overcome

Nov 9: Someone Who Inspires You

Nov 10: Something Someone Gave You

Nov 11: Color

Nov 12: Something You Use Every Day

Nov 13: Something You're Learning

Nov 14: A Memory

Nov 15: Your Age

Nov 16: Sounds

Nov 17: Creation or Nature

Nov 18: Hobbies

Nov 19: Accomplishment

Nov 20: Favorite Thing(s)

Nov 21: A Mentor or Teacher

Nov 22: Technology

Nov 23: Time

Nov 24: Something New or Old

Nov 25: Alone Time

Nov 26: On or Around the Table

Nov 27: Routine

Nov 28: This Place

Nov 29: Seasons

Nov 30: The Future

Just remember, there isn't one way to do this. These are just suggested prompts to get you started. If you think of something else to give thanks about, follow that.

Consider and Serve the Lonely

As we already touched on, there will be those who don't have anyone to spend this day with. Think about those in your life who might be all alone this year and consider inviting them into your gathering, the way Christ has done with us. Groups of people to consider:

- Those new to town (they might not be able to travel to see their family due to cost or convenience).
- Those without family in town or within driving distance. With Christmas just a few weeks following Thanksgiving, many people have to choose between the two when traveling back home or have guests come to see them.
- Single friends—this is a great group to do Friendsgiving with!
- Recently divorced or widowed. These friends will be having a very hard year, and it is a great opportunity to include them.
- Elderly—they might not be able to travel to see family or have family that can't travel to see them.

HOW TO MAKE THANKSGIVING *SET APART* FROM THE REST OF THE YEAR

These ideas aren't always overtly spiritual, nor do they have to be. They are simply ways you can make this holiday more intentional, memorable, and distinct during the year.

Gather with Others

Traditionally, gathering with others is something that is done on this day. Some of you may have more family than you know what to do with, having to divide this day up into several days of lots of feasting. Others of you may find yourself very much alone and feeling the pain of isolation on this day. Use this as an opportunity to find others to gather with. If you aren't physically or emotionally close to family, then start a Friendsgiving! There are likely others you know who aren't able to spend the day with family for various reasons. Be sure to let those in your life—friends, coworkers, and people at church—know that you will be alone this Thanksgiving and give them the opportunity to include you.

And if you can't gather with others this year, find a way to make it a special one for you. Set aside the day to focus on gratitude, maybe even making a list of 100 things you are grateful for. Oftentimes when we focus on what we do have, it helps us not feel the sting of what we don't have.

Be Present (Put Phones Down)

Phones are awesome in so many ways, but let's put them down on this day. A few years ago I made a basket and called it the phone jail. Now when people come for Thanksgiving, they have to drop the phone in the basket. They are welcome to grab it when they want to snap a pic. But they won't be tempted to mindlessly scroll their phones. Let's be fully engaged and making memories right where we are, instead of scrolling through everyone's best photographed memories on our phones.

Give Thanks before or during the Meal

Sometimes we can forget to share our gratitude with one another. Take some time and circle up before the meal, then go around and ask everyone to share one thing they want to give thanks for that year. Or, if you don't want the food to get cold, have this be the first thing people share once they sit down.

Thankful Tree

I have a few fake branches, but you could gather real branches, that I put in a vase in our living room. Next to it is a jar of craft leaves, Sharpies, and ribbon with a sign that says, "Give Thanks! Write one thing you are thankful for on the leaf and tie it to our tree!" When people come to your home, ask them to add a leaf to the tree. If you live with friends or family, remind them from time to time to add a leaf to the tree. This is my favorite fall decoration each year. I save the leaves and keep them in a bag with the branches and read through them each year.

Make a List of 100 Things

Grab a big sheet of paper or grab one hundred popsicle sticks and challenge the kids in your life to come up with one hundred things during the month of November that they are thankful for. Keep these on your table and go through them at mealtime and try to think of more. We want to encourage the kids in our lives to see things to be grateful for. Gratefulness is a mind-set that requires discipline. Let's pass this discipline on to the kids!

Give the Kids a Job

You want to invite the kids into feeling a part of this holiday. Most of the time kids are pushed out of the kitchen and then placed at the kids' table. Find a way to include kids in this day by giving them responsibilities. Have them cook or prep parts of the meal. Assign them to make homemade cards, set the table, or take drink orders. They will feel so special and they will take a lot more pride in the gathering when they've played a part in it.

MAKE IT *YOUR* SACRED HOLIDAY

What Are Some Ideas You've Heard of That Might Make This Holiday More Meaningful?

What Has Worked?

What Hasn't Worked?

What Do You Want to Try in the Future?

What Struggles Do You Need to Prepare For?

❑ **How to Not Be THAT Christian** *(read chapter 11)*

❑ **Realistic Expectations** *(read chapter 12)*

❑ **Conflict, Drama, and All the Feels** *(read chapter 13)*

❑ **Budgets and Generosity** *(read chapter 14)*

❑ **Schedules and Plans** *(read chapter 15)*

❑ **Grief** *(read chapter 16)*

❑ **Other:**

❑ **Other:**

❑ **Other:**

❑ **Other:**

Use the space below to list common struggles you experience for this holiday. Then take some time to list some possible solutions or things that aren't helpful. Be sure to come back here and update what worked and didn't after the holiday. Oftentimes struggles become less or more in our minds with time. This will help you handle these struggles realistically the next year.

SHARING CHALLENGE 📷 🐦

WE ALL WANT TO HEAR YOUR IDEAS! Share online what you are doing to prepare for Thanksgiving. Be sure to use *#sacredholidays* and tag *@sacredholidays* so we can all learn from you and join in on your holy and/or set apart idea!

CHAPTER 9

ADVENT AND CHRISTMAS

Christmas is often where people start their journey to making their holidays more sacred—holy and set apart. Ironic that it comes last on the calendar and is one of the final chapters in the holiday section of this book, because it is likely the reason you picked up this book. I hope this shows you that this isn't the only holiday that you can set apart to love God and love others well.

With that said, there is a reason this holiday is so special—it's the one when we celebrate the coming of Jesus! It's a seemingly simple story, a baby born in a manger, but it changed everything. This coming finally put a stop to the thousands of years that the Israelites waited for a Messiah. This coming broke the separation between God and man; before, the only access they had to the Father was through a priest. This coming fulfilled countless prophecies. This coming was anything but simple; it changed everything then and everything for us today!

This holiday has become hyper commercialized, and the cultural celebrations of the holidays has made it hard to find the origins of this day. On top of that, it's hard to not get caught up in the magic of the season. Most of us love this season and yet we really struggle to break from our traditions, our ways of doing things in the past, and forge a new way. While our culture is very much removing the celebration of Christ from Christmas, it has very little intention of removing Christmas. Sadly, the holiday is becoming mostly about parties, sweets, decorations, and a pile of presents that puts last year's to shame. We have gotten so very far from what this holiday is about.

I am so proud of you for taking steps to redeem it. Choosing to make this holiday more sacred is not an easy one. In fact, it might be the hardest one of all because oftentimes your choices toward sacred will feel like an affront to others, even others who believe the same as you. As we talk about in this book often, we can still celebrate Christ without becoming one of *those* Christians. Sometimes in our pursuit of sacred, we lose our joy and forget to love. Let's not do that this year.

My greatest advice to you, as it is throughout this book, is to ask the Lord what this holiday should look like for you. Remember that you are forming a sacred way and that won't happen overnight and be done perfectly in one season. One baby step at a time, one year after another.

WHY DO WE CELEBRATE CHRISTMAS?
WHAT IS ADVENT?

Christmas is all about celebrating the coming of Jesus. Choosing to participate in Advent is one of the best ways to do that because it's an intentional practice of focusing on His coming.

Traditionally Advent begins the four Sundays prior to Christmas Day. A very common practice during Advent is the use of Advent candles. You begin with five candles and light a candle each of the four Sundays leading up to Christmas, and then the final one on Christmas Day. This practice helps us to visually experience the coming of the Light of the World. Jesus said in John 8:12, "I am the light of the world. Whoever follows me will not walk in darkness, but will have the light of life." So we light candles to celebrate that His coming removes darkness and leads us to walk in the light of life. This is what we celebrate at Christmas—the Light has come!

But what do we do with all the other traditions? At the end of this book I discuss Santa in detail for those with littles, so we won't discuss that here. There are tons of other traditions and expectations that encompass this holiday, each different for each family. Some of those traditions feel like home and you just can't imagine parting with them. Good news—you don't have to! Not having an overtly spiritual connection to each and every tradition doesn't mean those traditions can't be sacred. For example, one of our favorite traditions each year is our annual cookie-decorating contest. On Christmas Eve we bake sugar cookies and get out all the decorating supplies. Then three generations gather around a table and decorate cookies for hours. We tease each other for the not-so-cute creations and applaud one another's when we have a creative genius moment. The kids are as into the competition as the grown-ups. After we are done we all pick our best ones, and we post them online for our friends and family to vote on. It has become a way of including others into our holidays, especially the Sacred Holidays online community. They choose the winner and then the winner gets bragging rights for the whole year. This year, my seven-year-old daughter legitimately won and it got a bigger smile out of her than any present she opened on Christmas morning. I share this to show you that anything can be made sacred.

Christmas activities can be intentionally spiritual, or they can not be, depending on the moment. After all, Jesus sometimes gathered in spaces with people He cared for and simply broke bread and talked, and other times He "went there" on a spiritual level. Oftentimes we try to over-spiritualize the holidays in an attempt to bring greater glory to God. While these intentions aren't bad at all, we must keep an eye on our tendency to religiously script certain moments in ways even Jesus didn't. In some sacred moments, we love God and others by verbally connecting an activity to the Bible or the Lord. In other sacred moments, we love God and others by simply enjoying an activity. Jesus' days were filled with both types of sacred moments! At the end of the day, only the Lord's leading can decide what's best for each activity you do.

However, remember, dear friend, you have nothing to prove to your Father, others, or yourself. You are already loved by Him just as you are. The Christmas story sets the stage for no pretense—it's a simple story of a baby born in a manger. He didn't come with the pomp and circumstance one would expect (with the exclusion of the best birth announcement ever to the shepherds). He was born in a place where animals were; there was no place for Him or His family in an inn. Even though His birth announcement was magical with a multitude of angels proclaiming, "Glory to God in the highest, and on earth peace among those with whom he is pleased!" (Luke 2:14), that proclamation was made to shepherds, the lowliest of the low of that day.

So come just as you are. Offer just what you have to offer this year. But most of all, let's celebrate because the wait is over—the Messiah has come!

WHY DO YOU CELEBRATE CHRISTMAS AND ADVENT?

Make Your Personal Christmas and Advent
MISSION STATEMENT

Write out what you want Christmas and Advent to be about (and not about). This is where you make what was just a holiday into a Sacred Holiday—holy and set apart. We will get to the details of how you will carry it out, but first start with what you want this season to be about.

IDEAS FOR A MORE SACRED ADVENT AND CHRISTMAS

Don't try to do all of these ideas or try to implement all the other ideas you've heard before. Take baby steps into each holiday. (Go back and read chapter 1 if you need this reminder.) Pick one or two things to try this year and do them really well. Make notes in the white spaces of what did and didn't work, so you have a customized resource for many years to come!

HOW TO MAKE ADVENT AND CHRISTMAS *HOLY*

Advent Bible Study

Using an Advent Bible study is my number one recommendation to anyone wanting less chaos and more Jesus during Christmas. There are many options for devotionals out there, but I would highly encourage you to use one that is more of a Bible study than devotional. The difference is that devotionals are usually focused on an individual's perspective or experience with a verse to go along with their thoughts. But Bible studies give you a great insight and understanding of Scripture itself. At Sacred Holidays, the ministry, we aim to provide new, biblically based content each year that intentionally pushes you into Scripture.

Regardless of whether you choose to do a Bible study or read through the Christmas story on your own, the important thing to remember is that His Word is alive (Heb. 4:12). We simply cannot expect to feel more connected to the Father apart from His Word. Christians are becoming far too comfortable listening to other people's thoughts on Scripture without learning to be a student of the Word on our own.

I know the holidays are crazy, but they aren't too crazy to make time for Bible study. At the beginning of each of our studies, I always ask our readers to write out three things they've done that is harder than doing a Bible study at Christmas time. Then

I remind them to give themselves grace. We are disciplined and make sacrifices to make that time a priority, but when we miss days (and we will all miss days), we don't wallow in shame. We receive the grace already given to us and we continue walking with our Father. We study His Word not to achieve something, but to connect with Him.

Finally, a few tips to help you make Bible study during Advent a reality:

- Pick something you will give up during Advent that takes up your time or attention. Or choose something you'll fast from until you've spent time with God that day. For me, I know that if I touch my phone in the morning before spending time with the Lord, then I will waste thirty minutes on Instagram. I wish I had better self-control than that, but I just don't. So I set a rule to not get on social media until I've spent time with the Lord. Find what would be the best motivator for you. Give yourself some flexibility with this in finding what works best for you. (Whatever is that thing you really don't want to admit that you should do, that's probably the thing you should do.)
- Put your time with God through Bible study on your calendar and keep the appointment. Again, this is a discipline, and just like you wouldn't think to miss your family's Christmas pictures or that meeting with your boss to get your holiday bonus, set this time with the Lord to be just as valuable.
- Do the study with a group. This is always the one I get the most pushback on and also the one I get the biggest thank-yous for at the end of each Advent. The first time I did it, I was super hesitant to say yes to it. I felt like this time of

year was already crazy enough, why in the world would I agree to a weekly meetup?! You know what? It ended up being one of my most favorite parts. It also helped me say no to things that I didn't really value because I had less free time. But the best part of all was getting to really process what the Lord was teaching me about Him and learning from others, too! I felt like I celebrated Him more than I ever had before!

Advent Candles

Using Advent candles is an easy way to focus more on the One who is coming during Christmas. The same whimsy you feel with the twinkle of Christmas lights, you will feel for the glow of your Advent candles. The reason we use Advent candles is to shift our focus to the Light of the World, which is Jesus, whose coming we are celebrating.

You have freedom to use whatever candles you'd like for your Advent candle display. You might have grown up in a church that used Advent candles, or you might be hearing about this practice for the first time here. Either way, this practice is for all denominations because it's a celebration of the Light! You will need five candles, but they can be any shape, size, or color. (In some churches you will see that they use certain colors for certain candles on certain weeks. This is a denominational preference and is in no way something you need to hold to for your home use. However, if that method works for you too, then use it—there is freedom!)

For lighting candles, you will begin by lighting the first candle four Sundays before Christmas, then light an additional candle each Sunday. The fifth and final candle is lit on Christmas morning. The Sacred Holidays' Advent studies will guide you through the lighting process, but this is something you can do on your own as well. Below is a suggestion of verses you can read for each lighting, but, again, make this your own each year! (And if you have kids, feel free to get them their own set of battery-powered Advent candles for their room so they can celebrate the coming of Christ in their own space.)

Recommended Light verses to read when lighting Advent candles:

- The First Candle (Four Sundays before Christmas):
  — Genesis 1:1–3: "In the beginning, God created the heavens and the earth. The earth was without form and void, and darkness was over the face of the deep. And the Spirit of God was hovering over the face of the waters. And God said, 'Let there be light,' and there was light."
  — Ephesians 5:8: "For at one time you were darkness, but now you are light in the Lord. Walk as children of light."
- The Second Candle (Three Sundays before Christmas):
  — Isaiah 42:16: "And I will lead the blind in a way that they do not know, in paths that they have not known I will guide them. I will turn the darkness before them into light, the rough places into level ground. These are the things I do, and I do not forsake them."
  — John 1:1–5: "In the beginning was the Word, and the Word was with God, and the Word was God. He was in the beginning with God. All things were made through him, and without him was not any thing made that was made. In him was life, and the life was the light of men. The light shines in the darkness, and the darkness has not overcome it."
- The Third Candle (Two Sundays before Christmas):

— Psalm 119:105, 130: "Your word is a lamp to my feet and a light to my path. . . . The unfolding of your words gives light; it imparts understanding to the simple."

— 1 Peter 2:9: "But you are a chosen race, a royal priesthood, a holy nation, a people for his own possession, that you may proclaim the excellencies of him who called you out of darkness into his marvelous light."

• The Fourth Candle (One Sunday before Christmas):

— Exodus 13:21: "And the LORD went before them by day in a pillar of cloud to lead them along the way, and by night in a pillar of fire to give them light, that they might travel by day and by night."

— John 1:9–14: "The true light, which gives light to everyone, was coming into the world. He was in the world, and the world was made through him, yet the world did not know him. He came to his own, and his own people did not receive him. But to all who did receive him, who believed in his name, he gave the right to become children of God, who were born, not of blood nor of the will of the flesh nor of the will of man, but of God. And the Word became flesh and dwelt among us, and we have seen his glory, glory as of the only Son from the Father, full of grace and truth."

• The Fifth Candle (Christmas morning):

— Isaiah 9:6: "For to us a child is born, to us a son is given; and the government shall be upon his shoulder, and his name shall be

called Wonderful Counselor, Mighty God, Everlasting Father, Prince of Peace."
— John 8:12: "Again Jesus spoke to them, saying, 'I am the light of the world. Whoever follows me will not walk in darkness, but will have the light of life.'"

Before you light the first candle, take note of the darkness. I recommend even going into the darkest place in your home, like a closet or bathroom. Notice how darkness makes you feel and confess to the Father that apart from Christ we are in total darkness—we can't see, we don't know our next step, and we are alone. Then note each week how the light changes things and how that correlates to how Christ's presence in your life changes things for you. As you pass the lights, thank your Father for being light and bringing light to your life.

Put the candles some place you pass or sit frequently, so you see them often. Also, consider, if it's allowed, having some at your place of work. Battery-operated candles are allowed most places and are an easy way to fix your heart on what matters at your desk; it would also be an easy conversation starter to share the Light with those you work with!

For further help: Watch this video about Advent candles: https://www.youtube.com/watch?v=-n5FEZrItcc

Ornaments That Tell the Story of Jesus or Celebrate Him

I've done this a few different ways in the past and found it helpful to shift my focus on the story of the One I was celebrating. You can do this many different ways. One very common way is to participate in the Jesse Tree. This is based off of the full story of Jesus traced throughout all of Scripture. Each day focuses on a different element of the story with a coordinating ornament. You can put this together for yourself, but I've also done it with groups where we each made twenty-five of the same ornament and then shared them with twenty-five other people.

Another way to celebrate with ornaments is making your own "names of God" ornaments. Each day you could choose a name you have for God—writing out who He has been to you or what you have seen Him do in Scripture.

There isn't one way to do this; choose what feels celebratory for you!

Go to Church

I know each of us has a different relationship with the church. Like most relationships, it is one that is tangled with rich beauty and deep pain. Some of you haven't set foot in a church in years, or at least not since last Christmas. I don't know your reason, and maybe you aren't sure either. Sometimes life just passes by and what we meant to do, just never gets done. Use this time to step back into the body of Christ. Know this church family is as messy as your own family, because we are all humans in desperate need of the One who came to save us. But as the early church modeled the importance of gathering together, we should practice this too. Yes, it's easier to sleep in and get a full weekend day for fun. But the better way is for us to gather together with others to read God's Word, pray, praise Him, and break bread. Let us not neglect this, and if we have, let's use this season to come back home.

Love like Jesus: Adopt a Person, Family, or Ministry

This is where you can be generous during the holidays! If you are able to give financially, there are many who can benefit from your generosity. Although, there are many ways to be generous, so don't limit yourself to just financial. If you aren't sure where to start, begin by looking up and around at those in your everyday life. Is there a single mom who could use a free night of babysitting so she can get shopping done or just a night of peace in the midst of the chaos? Is there a homeless person on the corner you could give a cup of hot coffee to and a blanket? Maybe a group of your friends could do a coat drive and collect jackets for a shelter for abused women. This is where you can get creative with your generosity. Let's make this season sacred by loving others well, and maybe in new ways.

A Memory Ornament

This was something that was recommended to me a couple of years ago, and it has become a favorite tradition! Each Christmas, pick out an ornament to celebrate something the Lord did in your life that past year. Keep a record of each ornament in a journal and the reason you chose it. Then each year, as you hang it on the tree, thank God again for who He was then and who He is still today. Let it serve as a reminder of what He has done and is doing in your life.

Act Out the Christmas Story

This is my favorite tradition to do with my kids, and it's one that evolves with time and is easy to adapt with every age. When my oldest daughter was a baby, I bought a little plastic nativity set. I would act out the story for her using the characters. As she got older and as my other girls were born, I would have them tell the story using those little plastic figurines.

This past year, we took it up a notch and acted it out like a play—they each played a part and we invited whoever was around to join in. Since they are getting older and have a fuller scope of the Bible and the gospel story, we backed up the story all the way to creation, in the beginning. We talked about God creating light from nothing, so they could connect the focus of light all the way to creation. The girls would cover their eyes and walk around like blind people. We went through the story of Adam and Eve and sin entering the world, revealing our need for a Savior. We talked about Satan and how he was so crafty then, and how he is still the father of lies today (John 8:44). The girls found it particularly hilarious to go from being naked and unashamed to then realizing they were naked. We flipped through the pages between Genesis to the Gospels and we shared about some of the prophecies about a coming Savior. They loved getting to yell out different prophecies. Then we got to Luke and went through each of the stories: Zechariah and Elizabeth, Mary and Joseph, the journey to Bethlehem, Jesus being born, the birth announcement to the shepherds, and then Jesus' visit from the Magi as a toddler.

They loved it, and I wanted to sob watching them get to understand Scripture in such a real way. The truth is, *I* understood it in a more real way watching them act it out, too. The thing with the play is it wasn't perfect. There were so many things I missed. I would leave out parts and I definitely added parts that weren't there a few times, as I narrated the skit for them. This doesn't have to be perfect. Give yourself grace as you lead this out. Let them be kids. Let them be silly with it and goof off during it. We want them to love telling the story instead of feeling forced to do this.

As your kids get older, I've heard of bigger kids acting it out all by themselves. I've heard of some families that even let the kids record it themselves, so they have a video to share each year. As your kids get older, give them more and more ownership over this. We want to empower them to be gospel storytellers! And if you aren't a parent, consider doing this as a Sunday school activity during Christmas time in a kids' class, or make it a fun Christmas activity if you are babysitting a group of little ones.

HOW TO MAKE ADVENT AND CHRISTMAS *SET APART* FROM THE REST OF THE YEAR

These ideas aren't always overtly spiritual, nor do they have to be. They are simply ways you can make this holiday more intentional, memorable, and distinct during the year.

Advent Calendar

An Advent calendar is a simple way to build expectation and excitement as you count down the coming of Jesus! You can make your own countdown chain, find a free downloadable calendar online, or find one to purchase. There are ones that are beautifully designed, and then there are ones where you pop a piece of chocolate out of a box each day. Again, this isn't exactly a spiritual thing; it's another way to fix your excitement on the countdown. Just like you likely count down to other important days in your life, let's count down to one of the most exciting days of the year!

Giving Gifts

If I'm being honest, this is the hardest tradition for me. I still don't know where I stand with it. I am a big believer in lavishing others with fun and goodies on their birthday, which you will read about in the next chapter, but I really struggle with this at Christmas. It feels off to give so much to others on a holiday that just isn't about others; it's about Jesus. Forgive me for sounding legalistic here. I just want to share that I, too, am on this journey of finding my way to a more sacred holiday. There are a few perspectives that have helped me continue with the gift-giving tradition.

First, as I've said before, sometimes there is something so sacred to things that aren't considered spiritual at all, and sometimes the most spiritual thing we can do is lavishly love others. One shift I've made has been to make gift giving more intentional. It's become less about the quantity and wow factor of the gift, and more about the meaning. I want the gift I give to someone to feel holy and set apart. My hope is that when they see or use it months from opening it, they feel loved. Loving others is sacred because it was a command from Jesus, the second greatest command (Matt. 22:39).

Second, and this feels like a bit of a reach to me, I've heard others say they follow the example of the wise men by giving three gifts to a special friend or family member, spouse, or children. I don't believe we need to justify it with this model, but I do think it is a great way to reinforce the story with children, and also to help us keep giving in moderation.

Third, we give based off of the model of St. Nicholas. I love the tradition of St. Nicholas, which I discuss in the Santa chapter (see page 229). Since our culture is all about Santa, I find it easy to get to share about St. Nicholas. While we don't know if any of the legends of St. Nicholas are true, the model is beautiful. He was a rich man who was extremely generous with the poor.

When it comes to giving, let's make our focus not on the "have to" of giving the gift, but the "get to"—we get to love these people. Here are a few tips that will help the process feel more loving than something we are bound to by obligation:

- Keep a list of people you want to buy gifts for on your phone (or in a journal if you are a paper girl); make notes throughout the year of thoughtful things for them, or things they mention.
- Buy gifts before Advent begins. I know this sounds a little crazy, but this is something I started doing a few years ago and it has freed me up and relieved me of so much stress. I still buy stocking stuffers and a few miscellaneous gifts here and there, but most are purchased before Advent begins.
- Set a budget and stick to it. See the chapter on budgets and generosity for more tips. Know this one is a hard one for me because I love shopping and love lavishing others with things. Going into debt over gifts isn't something that is worth it. As we shift our value in giving gifts, it's not about the wow factor, but the meaning. If money is tight or nonexistent, give coupon books, a thoughtful letter, or something homemade.

A special note for parents, guardians, and influencers of kids to read before you read the ideas below:

This isn't something that is easy to say, but something I'm going to say because I love you. This Christmas cannot be all about the kids. I don't mean it just in the "giving them too many gifts" kind of a way; I mean it even in the spiritual context. I get you, I am you. A mom, with three young kids, who wants more than anything for my kids to know Jesus and follow Him. With good intentions we can make these obviously sacred holidays all about opportunities to teach our kids. Yes, we should always seek opportunities to show them the gospel. However, and this is a big however, it should never come ahead of our own pursuit of Christ. We cannot lead our kids where we are not currently walking. We cannot make disciples if we aren't disciples ourselves. I get a lot of questions from moms about how they can do Advent with their kids. And my response is always this: Advent is for you first, then it is for your child. Just as the flight attendant encourages you to put your mask on first then your child's, so I encourage you in the same way. You must first celebrate Advent, then invite your kids into it. I don't mean that you can't involve your kids in it this year if it's your first shot at celebrating Advent. I simply mean to be sure you don't exclusively try this list of things to do with your kids and neglect what you can do first. Most of what I share for adults are all things that can be incorporated for the whole family to participate in. The beauty is that they get to see us do it first; the disciple gets to watch the discipler show them how, not just tell them how. Let's lead our kids to celebrate Jesus from a place of celebrating Jesus ourselves! This is the best way you can lead your kids.

For further help, watch this video: https://www. youtube.com/watch?v=AS8qVKTQ5co&t=3s

Don't Make Wish Lists, Make Gift Lists

Whether you do Santa or not, I highly encourage parents to not focus on building wish lists for Christmas. As their parent, you likely already know what they want (and if you don't, there will be plenty of opportunities to hear without you asking for a list). The reason why I don't ever have my kids make a wish list is because I don't want them focused at all on what they get.

Instead, we focus on what we give. So they make a list of the people they want to give gifts to and I try as often as possible to steer their thoughts around what they want to give others that year. The reason for this, as you already know, is that every single person in their life will ask them what they want for Christmas (or what they want Santa to bring them). So, instead, we choose not to center our conversations on their wish lists for what they'd like to get, but rather on what they'd like to give.

With this in mind, since this section is for all of us with kids in our lives, let's shift our wording from being centered around asking kids the default, "What do you want for Christmas?" Instead, ask questions like: "Who are you most excited to give a gift to this year?" Or, if it's after Christmas, "What was your favorite gift to give this year?"

Dollar Store Christmas

I've already shared that I have a really hard time with how the gift-giving piece fits into Christmas, given that the holiday is about exalting Jesus and not about exalting someone else, the way a birthday is. I struggle here, but at the same time, I do generally love giving gifts, and I think it's a good thing to show generosity. Weighing it all out, we've decided as a family to give gifts at Christmas time, given that the cultural expectation of generosity during this holiday is something we enjoy, and also is a way to put Christ's generosity on display. It was important for me to train my girls to be generous and thoughtful gift givers.

Chris and I both come from divorced homes, so we have a lot of family members. For us to buy a few gifts for each of our girls plus all the family is a lot. Then for our girls to buy a gift for them too was more than our budget could handle. One thing I started doing when Karis (my oldest) was a toddler, was taking her to the dollar store to pick out a gift for each person in our extended family. This has allowed each of our girls to buy gifts for the twenty-plus family members we see at Christmas and give them a personally picked gift, without it costing us a ton of money. When we see family now, they are just as excited to give gifts as to get them.

We make a list before we go to the store of everyone in our family, plus they can each pick one friend too. Then they can pick one thing for each person. We talk through what things that person might want. For the youngest ones, I often have to use the phrase, "Is this something *you* would want or *they* would want?" After that, I let them completely pick the gift. Because it's just cute when your three-year-old gives their grandpa a *Woman's World Crossword Puzzle* book and your father-in-law some Barbie hair spray.

Happy Birthday Jesus Party

What kid doesn't love an excuse for a birthday party? This is a super easy (and fun!) way to help kids realize that this day is all about Jesus' birthday. You can do this before Christmas and let your kids invite a bunch of people over for a full-out birthday party. If you do this, go all out, just like you would if it was one of your kids' birthday parties. Or you can keep it simple and make a cake as a family on Christmas Day.

Empower your kids to make a gift for Him. Don't put any limitations on this—let them be them. This past year my oldest made Jesus a birthday card, a drawing of the two of them under a rainbow, and a list of one hundred things she loved about Him. She did all this without me asking her to. I don't share this to brag, but to encourage you, that all your hard efforts will pay off. So, for the years we are able, let's encourage them to celebrate Him in hopes that a love for celebrating the One who has come is the thing they value most this time of year.

Fund-raiser for a Cause

We have many friends who do this with their children. This can be done a few ways—they collect things or raise money for a specific cause. We have a neighbor who is very involved in homeless ministry. Her family has learned that the homeless desperately need bikes so they can get to and from job interviews and then to jobs they've secured. They heard of this need and then collected more than fifty bikes in a week! We have other family friends who empower their kids to choose a cause to donate to. They let their kids come up with something to sell—whether it's a product they make or a service. Then on Christmas Eve they have their kids put their money under the tree. When they wake up in the morning, their money's gone and the parents set up a display symbolizing what their money will provide for the cause they contributed to. This hands-on experience teaches kids exactly what following Jesus' example means during Christmas; Jesus saw our helpless condition, came close to us, and did something about it. We do the same for others!

MAKE IT *YOUR* SACRED HOLIDAY

What Are Some Ideas You've Heard of That Might Make This Holiday More Meaningful?

What Has Worked?

What Hasn't Worked?

What Do You Want to Try in the Future?

What Struggles Do You Need to Prepare For?

❑ **How to Not Be THAT Christian** *(read chapter 11)*

❑ **Realistic Expectations** *(read chapter 12)*

❑ **Conflict, Drama, and All the Feels** *(read chapter 13)*

❑ **Budgets and Generosity** *(read chapter 14)*

❑ **Schedules and Plans** *(read chapter 15)*

❑ **Grief** *(read chapter 16)*

❑ **Other:**

❑ **Other:**

❑ **Other:**

❑ **Other:**

Use the space below to list common struggles you experience for this holiday. Then take some time to list some possible solutions or things that aren't helpful. Be sure to come back here and update what worked and didn't after the holiday. Oftentimes struggles become less or more in our minds with time. This will help you handle these struggles realistically the next year.

SHARING CHALLENGE 📷 🐦

WE ALL WANT TO HEAR YOUR IDEAS! Share online what you are doing to prepare for Christmas. Be sure to use *#sacredholidays* and tag *@sacredholidays* so we can all learn from you and join in on your holy and/or set apart idea!

CHAPTER 10

HAPPY BIRTHDAY

You know that I don't love how commercialized we've made most holidays, and how I don't know where I stand on giving gifts at Christmas since it makes it all about others instead of the One we should be celebrating. But, I know exactly where I stand when it comes to birthdays—it is all about the birthday person! And I do mean *all* about them. This is the one day—or as we like to do in our family, the one week—when we can make it all about that person.

WHY DO WE CELEBRATE BIRTHDAYS?

We celebrate birthdays because it is the day of that person's birth—it's when we celebrate their life! We celebrate birthdays because we are celebrated and adored by our Father. Not only does He call us valuable and knows every hair on our head (Luke 12:7), but He created us and knows us.

> O Lord, you have searched me and known me! You know when I sit down and when I rise up; you discern my thoughts from afar. You search out my path and my lying down and are acquainted with all my ways. Even before a word is on my tongue, behold, O Lord, you know it

altogether. You hem me in, behind and before, and lay your hand upon me. Such knowledge is too wonderful for me; it is high; I cannot attain it. . . . For you formed my inward parts; you knitted me together in my mother's womb. I praise you, for I am fearfully and wonderfully made. Wonderful are your works; my soul knows it very well. My frame was not hidden from you, when I was being made in secret, intricately woven in the depths of the earth. Your eyes saw my unformed substance; in your book were written, every one of them, the days that were formed for me, when as yet there was none of them. How precious to me are your thoughts, O God! How vast is the sum of them! If I would count them, they are more than the sand. (Ps. 139:1–6, 13–18)

This is the one time of year we should go above and beyond to celebrate the birthday person!

WHY DO YOU CELEBRATE BIRTHDAYS?

Make Your Personal Birthday
MISSION STATEMENT

Write out what you want your birthday and others' birthdays to be about (and not about). This is where you make what was just a holiday into a sacred holiday—holy and set apart. We will get to the details of how you will carry it out, but first start with what you want this season to be about.

IDEAS FOR A MORE SACRED BIRTHDAY

Don't try to do all of these ideas or try to implement all the other ideas you've heard before. Take baby steps into each holiday. (Go back and read chapter 1 if you need this reminder.) Pick one or two things to try this year and do them really well. Make notes in the white spaces of what did and didn't work, so you have a customized resource for many years to come!

HOW TO MAKE BIRTHDAYS *HOLY*

Delight in the Father's Love for You

At the start of your birthday, spend some time listening to your Father. Search in the Bible for verses about the Father's love for you. Ask Him to tell you what He says is true about you and write those words out. Let the Spirit speak words that are true and loving over you. Take time to remember that He gave you the gift of life and has plans for you. Whether or not you feel adored or noticed this birthday by others, starting this way will help you fill up on God's delight in you before you enter into the attention of others!

Reflect and Dream

When it's your birthday, set aside some time the week before or after to reflect and dream. Block off an hour or longer, so you don't feel rushed.

Think about the past year. What were some successes to celebrate and thank the Father for? Are there any failures you need to grieve or confess? Do you have any regrets or missed opportunities? What about moments you are really proud of?

Now, think about the year to come. Ask the Father to give you courage to dream bigger for this year than you would think possible on your own. Ask Him to show you what's next. Ask Him for clear vision for the very next step and full faith for all the steps to follow. Write out any steps or visions He might give you. List out any goals you'd like to achieve this next year, along with some practical first steps to get started. Think about your life in several categories: physical body, spiritual, emotional and relational, professional, and whatever other categories fit.

HOW TO MAKE BIRTHDAYS *SET APART* FROM THE REST OF THE YEAR

These ideas aren't always overtly spiritual, nor do they have to be. They are simply ways you can make this holiday more intentional, memorable, and distinct during the year.

Share Your Favorite Things about the Birthday Person

This is my very favorite thing to do for others on their birthday, and I hope it becomes a favorite tradition of yours as well. When it is someone's birthday, I love to celebrate that person specifically by taking a minute or two to let them know what I specifically love about them and am grateful for regarding their life.

If this is an old friend on social media, take the time and leave more than a typical "happy birthday" comment. It takes forty-five seconds more to write something you see in that person or love about them. If it's a friend that you have an actual phone number for, send them a text or call them to tell what you love about them. People get tons of messages on social media and text messages on their birthday and they are, mostly, the same. Be different; celebrate them specifically!

Then take it one step further for your real-life friends and family who you gather around a table with on their birthday. Encourage everyone to go around the table to celebrate that person. Look them in the eye. Don't rush. Tell them all the ways you are proud of them and all the dreams you have for them this next year. These words will likely be one of the most treasured gifts they receive that year. If someone isn't able to attend, ask them beforehand to share something with you and read it to the birthday person.

And this goes for kiddos too! We have done this on each of our kid's birthdays since they turned one—both at our family dinner on their birthday and each of their birthday parties. Chris or I will start it and then we invite our guests to share, then one of us will wrap it up. It is so sweet to invite kids to share what their favorite thing is about our daughters. Be sure to have a friend film this so you and your child can treasure these moments for years to come.

Do All of the Birthday Person's Favorite Things

As we've already said, this day is all about the birthday person. So on this day, let it be all about what that person wants to eat and do.

And if it's your birthday, and others are trying to make it all about you, let them. You might relish in it! But so many of you feel so out of place when people make too much of you. On this day, please, dear one, let them. Let others honor you and make it all about you.

All about the Birthday Kid

Just as we want to make it all about the birthday grown-up, we want to be all about the birthday kid. Form special traditions that your family can carry on for years and years. I asked our Sacred Holidays private Facebook group what made their birthday special. It was so fun to hear all the things that made their birthdays feel special, and most were really inexpensive. One person shared how her mom always laid out a lace tablecloth, many got to eat off of a special plate the whole day, others got to choose meals, and some got to choose whatever they wanted that day. I still haven't heard anyone mention a present. Don't get me wrong, I'm sure everyone has loved the presents they have received, because who doesn't like gifts? But these responses showed me that it was the little, consistent, and special ways we pay attention to others on their birthday that sticks with them for a lifetime.

I do this by staying up late the night before my kid's birthday. I try to decorate the downstairs as if we are having a birthday party the next day. Typically we don't have a party on their actual birthday and I like it even better that way. They know I'm doing it just for them, not for the party attendees. Then the rest of the day is the birthday girl's choice about everything. Chris and I say yes to just about everything because it's the one day of the year dedicated to celebrating all the ways God has uniquely made her—her tastes, preferences, and favorite activities included!

Half Birthdays

For kids, the half birthday is a big deal. There is some level of street cred that they must get on the playground once they can finally say their age and the "and a half" addition. So, in our family, we celebrate the day they get to add the "and a half." It's nothing over the top, but I try to make that day just a little bit special around meal time. We don't do gifts on this day or decorations, just a fun breakfast and then they get to pick out dinner or we go for cupcakes or ice cream after school. Occasionally I'll get something super small at the store for them or pick up flowers. Again, we don't go over the top.

It's easy to remember if you just set it on your calendar as a recurring event, just like any other birthday. Then I have an alert go off the day before and morning of.

Milestone Birthdays

Many families will do big things on milestone birthdays. Our kids haven't reached the age of getting to cash in on one of these yet, but we have begun to dream about this, considering things like future budget and expectations. Some things we have discussed: ten-year-old trip with Dad, thirteen-year-old get a phone, fifteen-year-old trip with Mom, and Sweet 16 (we will go half-in by matching what they save up to buy their own car). We aren't quite sure if we will do these things, but these are goals we are starting to set and will need to adjust our budget to accommodate for. Determine what birthdays you want to become a milestone for your kids, and plan to pump up that day in order to celebrate them.

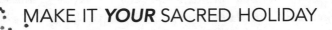

MAKE IT *YOUR* SACRED HOLIDAY

What Are Some Ideas You've Heard of That Might Make This Holiday More Meaningful?

What Has Worked?

What Hasn't Worked?

What Do You Want to Try in the Future?

What Struggles Do You Need to Prepare For?
- ❑ **How to Not Be THAT Christian** *(read chapter 11)*
- ❑ **Realistic Expectations** *(read chapter 12)*
- ❑ **Conflict, Drama, and All the Feels** *(read chapter 13)*
- ❑ **Budgets and Generosity** *(read chapter 14)*
- ❑ **Schedules and Plans** *(read chapter 15)*
- ❑ **Grief** *(read chapter 16)*
- ❑ **Other:**

❑ **Other:**

❑ **Other:**

❑ **Other:**

Use the space below to list common struggles you experience for this holiday. Then take some time to list some possible solutions or things that aren't helpful. Be sure to come back here and update what worked and didn't after the holiday. Oftentimes struggles become less or more in our minds with time. This will help you handle these struggles realistically the next year.

SHARING CHALLENGE 📷 🐦

WE ALL WANT TO HEAR YOUR IDEAS! Share online what you are doing to prepare for birthdays. Be sure to use *#sacredholidays* and tag *@sacredholidays* so we can all learn from you and join in on your holy and/ or set apart idea!

PART 3

COMMON
Struggles

(READ AS NEEDED)

CHAPTER 11

HOW TO NOT BE *THAT* CHRISTIAN

This is one of the most tender chapters in this book because it is such a personal one. As we talk with many women at Sacred Holidays (the ministry), the topics in this chapter come up again and again. They are marked with a lot of confusion, fear, and insecurity. So let me say a couple things before we get started:

First, there isn't a right answer. This chapter is every shade of gray. I wish the topic of being "that" Christian was black and white, and many of us believe that it is black and white. However, this is simply one of those topics we have to take what we see in Scripture and apply it to our current context. And as we live a life of faith in the Father who loves us, we ask Him to show us the best way. We will likely change our shade of gray as our perspectives, wisdom, and circumstances change. What I hope to do for you in this chapter is to stretch your perspective just slightly.

Second, keep an open mind, even if you don't like or agree with what I've said. There aren't actual verses that spell out how to specifically approach the holidays. I hope I can show you what the Lord is teaching me from my journey through Scripture and life experiences.

As you see each perspective from different points of view, hopefully you'll be more equipped to make choices that are best for you. Just as we take baby steps into our practice of the holidays, we take baby steps into our perspective of the holidays.

It's a good thing to know which camp you fall into. Are you one of *those* people? Are you a little too caught-up in the whimsy? Are you wandering somewhere in the middle, a solid mid-tone gray?

HOW TO KNOW IF YOU ARE ONE OF *THOSE* PEOPLE

We all know *those* people. Likely, at least once, we've each been one of them too. The ones who swing the pendulum just a smidge too far when it comes to choosing more Jesus during the holidays. (If you just cringed because I just said holidays instead of Christmas or Easter, then this chapter will likely make you uncomfortable. It's okay; let's be uncomfortable for just a little bit.)

So who are *those* people? Before I tell you about them, I want to confess that I have felt many of these ways or done each of these things at certain points in my Christian walk. So this is not an accusatory list, but one that hits a little close to home. I hope we can identify the ways we have been *those* people . . . and I hope you laugh at yourself just a little too.

Those people are the ones who feel very passionate that Santa is just Satan spelled wrong. They are the ones who boycott all the stores at Christmas and not because they hate the crowds; they think each of those stores are anti-Christmas, so they will not give them their dollars. They are the ones who are offended when someone says "Happy Holidays." They are the ones who say or think we've taken Christ out of Christmas when we write X-mas. They are the ones who keep the porch light off on Halloween or think the only safe option is their church's Fall Festival. They are the ones who say "no presents, please" on their kid's birthday invites because they don't want to promote materialism. They are the ones who get a little annoyed and think, *Where have you been all year?* when the church parking lot is crowded at Easter, instead of thanking God that lost souls have the chance to hear the gospel, if even for a day. They are the ones who have a hard time letting others celebrate them on their birthday! They are the ones who feel like it's their personal cause to not let Thanksgiving be skipped over and refuse to even hum "Jingle Bells" until the turkey has been carved and eaten. They are the ones whose demeanors around the holidays are more marked by crossed arms than open ones, scowls rather than smiles, and complaints rather than creativity.

Are we still friends? Hopefully you laughed thinking about all the others who have been this way and hopefully you laughed a little at yourself, too.

I hesitated to share that at one time I was guilty of each of these things because I didn't want you to judge me or think that I am one of those people. Isn't that ridiculous? But our fear of admitting our wrong ways of thinking and living is what keeps us from freedom. So let's just own our silly ways of having done things.

The truth is that Jesus spent more words on rebuking the spiritually elite who refused to engage with the culture around them at all than rebuking those who were steeped in the sin of the culture. For many of us, we have been in a church bubble with our man-made Christian rules so long, we forgot the difference between a biblical truth and a cultural belief. We hold on to these ideologies and approaches that simply aren't in Scripture or its collective context.

To those who struggle to honor all the holy of the holidays but refuse the side that can be memorable and fun without being overly spiritual, I want you to experience the freedom that comes with having both.

HAVE YOU BECOME TOO RELIGIOUS?

When it comes to being overly religious about the holidays, sometimes our reasoning can be completely understandable. I have zero desire to debate or try to convince you to change the way you are doing things. But I hope today you pause for just a moment and ask yourself why you've come to these conclusions about some of the holidays. I hope today you open yourself up to letting your Father show you places that have started to become more about law-keeping than love.

How Have You Become Too Religious with Each of These Holidays?

(Note: Reflect on ways you may have become too religious around each of these holidays. If you aren't sure, you could even ask some family or friends you trust to be honest and loving with you. You may not have an example for each holiday. Again, this is something you will come back to again and again. You can add as the Spirit reveals it.)

NEW YEAR'S:

_____

_____

VALENTINE'S DAY:

_____

_____

LENT AND EASTER:

_____

_____

SUMMER:

_____

_____

HALLOWEEN:

_____

_____

THANKSGIVING:

_____

_____

ADVENT AND CHRISTMAS:

_____

_____

HAPPY BIRTHDAY (INCLUDING YOUR BIRTHDAY AND OTHERS):

_____

_____

Why Do You Think You Tend to Be Too Religious? What's at the Root of It?

HOW TO KNOW IF YOU ARE A LITTLE TOO WHIMSY

There are actually two types of _those_ Christians. We are already familiar with the first type; the second, however, we don't typically classify as being one of _those_ Christians. Surprisingly, it is my concern that this group makes up the majority of Christians in our current and upcoming generations. This type can be a lot more pleasant to be around, but that doesn't make it a better extreme.

We love your Christmas sweaters and how you put up your tree on November 1. Sure, we stand strong in our belief that you shouldn't skip past Thanksgiving, but since you've been all-things-pumpkin since September 1, we understand that you are ready for some red and green in your life. You have this way of making people's birthdays the most special day on the planet. You go to every single birthday party you are invited to and are sure to pick out an awesome gift for each. You have not just one tradition for each holiday; you have ten. While you are super pleasant to be around during the holidays, you can get a little too wrapped up in the whimsy of each holiday. You totally celebrated them and made some really fun memories.

The only problem is afterwards, you wonder if you missed Christ in the midst of all your celebrating. Maybe you didn't grow up in a family that focused on Jesus and you simply don't know what to do or where to begin. Or maybe you grew up in one of *those* other homes and you just want the opposite experience now. However, you ended up here, it seems you have focused on the "set apart" side of the holidays, making them intentional and memorable, which is great. However, I want you to know that things can be just as whimsical by focusing on Jesus. You can have set apart *and* holy. I promise you won't become one of *those* people in this process.

HAVE YOU BECOME TOO RELEVANT?

We live in a very complicated age to be a follower of Christ. With the rise of social media and how we all know each other's business all the time (or at least the parts we choose to put out there for others, real or perceived), we are under constant scrutiny. One wrong post and we are slaughtered; one relevant post and we are praised.

I see this pull for the Gen-X generation as well as the Millennials—to focus so much on being loving and living like

Jesus in a relevant way. This is a beautiful and noble ambition. We saw the generation ahead of us and felt that many valued religion over relationship, and we want to present a different narrative of the gospel. We want to provide a seat at the table for all people to explore Christ and His claims. We want great meaning attached to all we do. We want to be as authentic as possible.

Here's the problem with that: as we focus so much on others, we lose focus on the One who we are following. We want so desperately to create a space and a conversation that we miss the very clear standard laid out for us in the Word of God. We want to debunk every religious principle and replace it with truth, but instead we just replace it with a deep-thought meme. We interpret the gospel message through the eyes and words of our favorite teachers, writers, podcasters, and influencers. Many of us, not all of us, are getting further from the Word. We spend more time setting up our quiet time for our Instagram feeds than actually studying the Scriptures. We listen to podcasts more than we listen to the Holy Spirit. If we are honest, we still don't really know how to consistently study the Bible or pray on our own. We have a hard time deciphering what is true and what *sounds* like it would be true of Jesus.

We've summed up our mission in life, as followers of Jesus, to love others and love God. That's what He said to do, right (Matt. 22:36–40)? But instead of letting Scripture, wisdom, and the Spirit lead the application of this, we've allowed our culture to define it. Never wanting to offend, we filter out more Jesus than we've even realized because we want so much to be relevant.

Your intentions are pure, my friend. However, there is a better way.

How Have You Become Too Relevant with Each of These Holidays?

(Note: If you aren't sure how or even if you've become too relevant, ask some fellow followers of Christ who know you. This might be a good time to give your very conservative—socially and spiritually—friends and family members an open invite for opinions. You may not have an example for each holiday. Again, this is something you will come back to again and again. You can add as the Spirit reveals it.)

NEW YEAR'S:

_____

_____

VALENTINE'S DAY:

_____

_____

LENT AND EASTER:

_____

_____

SUMMER:

_____

_____

HALLOWEEN:

_____

_____

THANKSGIVING:

_____

_____

ADVENT AND CHRISTMAS:

_____

_____

**HAPPY BIRTHDAY (INCLUDING YOUR
BIRTHDAY AND OTHERS):**

_____

_____

**Why Do You Think You Tend to Be Too Relevant? What's at the Root
of It?**

SOMEWHERE IN THE MIDDLE

You may still be struggling to identify which one of _those_
Christians you are, or maybe you are like me and you are equal
parts both (we are such overachievers). You feel like you are both
too religious and at other times too relevant, or maybe you think
that makes you perfectly balanced.

I think we're the type of Christians who tend to be more religious, similar to the Pharisees. The Pharisees were always making
sure things were on point. They followed that law perfectly. The
world was only black and white, and nothing could be gray. They
could not possibly see a different way. I believe at their core they
meant well. They were given the law and aimed to follow it. I
believe that is what most of us are doing with the holidays when
we tend to resemble _those_ religious Christians. We have good

intentions and just want to make sure Jesus isn't lost in all the cultural and commercial celebrations. I adore your heart to protect the name of Christ and avoid what is evil. But let's remember that Jesus rebuked the Pharisees, and the Pharisees rejected Jesus. They were so focused on the law that they missed the One who is love. May we never hold on so tight to law that we forget to love.

I also think we're the type of Christians who tend to be more relevant, similar to Peter. Peter is one of my favorite people in Scripture because I relate to him most. He is a hot mess, but man, did he persist in following Jesus even though he got it wrong so many times. There is hope for us who are *those* relevant Christians. Jesus told Peter that he would deny Him at the end, and Peter did not believe that it could happen. But as the crowds cheered against Jesus, Peter was quiet. Not wanting to stir the pot or to stand out, he stayed quiet. He blended in. And then when really pushed, he even denied Jesus (Luke 22:54–62). My fear for those of us who lean this way is that we are following Peter's example and we don't even realize it. We don't notice that all our loving and relevant approaches are really just subtle ways of denying Christ. We want so badly for everyone to come to the table to hear the gospel that we fill our tables but never share what is true.

HE HAS CHOSEN YOU FOR NEW THINGS

God's Word may not specifically lay out how to handle the holidays, but it does tell us how He sees us and what He has called us to. Isaiah 42:1–17 is one of my favorites to read in this context of wanting to leave behind an old way of approaching holidays and starting a new way.

> Behold my servant, whom I uphold, my chosen, in whom my soul delights; I have put my Spirit upon him; he will bring forth justice to the nations. He will not cry aloud or lift up his voice, or make it heard in the street; a bruised reed he will not break, and a faintly burning wick he will not quench; he will faithfully bring forth justice. He will

not grow faint or be discouraged till he has established justice in the earth; and the coastlands wait for his law. Thus says God, the LORD, who created the heavens and stretched them out, who spread out the earth and what comes from it, who gives breath to the people on it and spirit to those who walk in it: "I am the LORD; I have called you in righteousness; I will take you by the hand and keep you; I will give you as a covenant for the people, a light for the nations, to open the eyes that are blind, to bring out the prisoners from the dungeon, from the prison those who sit in darkness. I am the LORD; that is my name; my glory I give to no other, nor my praise to carved idols. Behold, the former things have come to pass, and new things I now declare; before they spring forth I tell you of them." . . . And I will lead the blind in a way that they do not know, in paths that they have not known I will guide them. I will turn the darkness before them into light, the rough places into level ground. These are the things I do, and I do not forsake them. (Isa. 42:1–9, 16)

Over time the Lord will lead you out of being *that* Christian who is too religious or *that* Christian who is too relevant. He will not forsake you; He will not leave you to figure this out alone. He will lead us in His Word. But He will also lead us through one another. I hope this book is one of the ways He shows you a new way—a way that turns darkness into light. I hope He uses the #sacredholidays community to open your eyes. We get to be a part of what God is doing in the lives of one another.

LET'S NOT BE *THAT* OR *THAT* CHRISTIAN

As we've learned you can be *that* Christian by being too religious or *that* Christian by being too relevant. Let's aim for neither. Instead let's find our way to follow the Father, trust Jesus, study the Bible, and then listen to the Spirit as we find a healthy rhythm with our holidays.

Take a moment and write out a prayer confessing how you've been one of "those" Christians and one of "those" . . . Ask your Father to lead you down a new way on level ground:

CHAPTER 12

REALISTIC EXPECTATIONS

I always imagined each holiday would go a little differently than what became my reality. I can be a bit of an extreme person and I set really high expectations for myself, for others, and, yes, even for holidays. In my head I know what they could be, and the perfectionist, the overachiever in me just does not like it when reality falls short of ideal. The Hallmark Channel doesn't help either, with its constant stream of idealist movies that focus on each season all year long (which I absolutely adore).

The problem with this mind-set, and movie marathons, is that it can leave us awfully disappointed the majority of the time. When we hold our high expectations next to our very normal reality, we will be frustrated.

IT'S NOT THE WHOLE STORY

Before social media, we didn't really even know the extent to which people embraced the holidays unless we talked to a real-life friend or read an article somewhere. Even then, we usually knew the person outside of their social media persona and all that went into making their holiday so magical. Or when flipping through magazines, we were able to correctly identify that this was staged and pulled together for a magazine.

It's not so easy these days. With one press of a button and some swiping with our thumbs, we can quickly see that it seems like the entire world is doing holidays the "right way." Or take our beloved Hallmark movie marathons, with their perfectly staged settings, perfectly scripted actors, perfectly coiffed hair, and a perfectly happily-ever-after ending. This is not reality.

We forget when we watch TV or scroll through social media that what we see isn't real. Or if it is real, it isn't the whole truth.

We have to fight this comparison trap. Remember that you don't see the whole story in that perfectly staged image. They may rock at throwing birthday parties for friends or celebrating Advent with their family, but you don't know what they've sacrificed in order to do that. To say yes means we must first say no.

The other day I was interviewed for a podcast and they were asking me how I run a ministry, write a book, speak at women's events, and have three young kids at home. I told them life is about choices; we all have the same hours in our day. What people will never see me post on social media is a perfect meal plan, or even a full fridge. The truth is, I drive through Chick-fil-A more times than I'd like to admit for family meals; I use curbside pickup at the grocery store in order to remember to eat fruits and veggies; I don't work out nearly as much as I want to; I hardly ever clean (I have to pay someone to deep clean once a month!); and I don't get the chance to take all the different opportunities most moms can at their kids' school (like being a room mom—I've always wanted to do that and just can't right now!).

But here is the deal: I am better for the choices I'm learning to make. I am doing exactly what I most feel called to do, and it's because I am learning to say no to all the little good things that may not be my best things. I'm a better friend to my real-life friends because I don't try to socialize with everyone or spend a ton of time posting on or scrolling through social media. I am more present with my kids when they get home from school because I say no to other things during the day, and that helps me get my work done while they're gone. I still have a long way to go, a very long way, but I'm learning that what you see on social media isn't the whole story.

You may think when you scroll social media that it's possible to keep up with the facade because you see this woman doing this or another woman doing that. It's just not real. Yes, they are posting something real, and we should celebrate with our friends. But know that pulling off that dreamy cookie decorating party meant piles of dishes, sugar-crazed kids at bedtime, and a bonus three pounds on the scale the next day (all conveniently absent from her post).

So let's take our eyes off of what everyone else seems to be doing and focus more on what God says *we* should be doing.

YOU CAN ONLY EXPECT WHAT OTHERS CAN OFFER

Being a first-time mom wasn't easy. I wish so badly I was a baby person, but I'm just not. Don't get me wrong, I love babies and will circle new moms like a shark when they bring a baby into my presence. I also am obsessed with my kids, obviously, and had a really hard time putting them down. However, the baby stage wasn't my favorite. I know most moms yearn for those days, but I am just not that mom. Bring on the big kids, even the terrible twos because little toddler tantrums are hilarious to me. What's not hilarious to me is all the crying newborns do and then all the sleeping. Oddly enough, the seasons with little bitties were the most overstimulating and understimulating times of my entire life.

Then one day a friend gave me some of the best advice that I now apply to all life situations: "Becky, you need to just expect that she (my baby) will be a baby today. That's all. Expect nothing more and nothing less. Babies cry on average for three hours a day, sleep for sixteen hours a day, and eat six to eight times a day. Expect that to be your average."

I don't know why this blew my mind as a new mom, but it totally did. It helped me realize that for all but five hours of our day, my baby would either be asleep or crying, and never in a typical pattern. Then for those remaining five hours my baby would want to eat six to eight times. I still didn't love the screaming cries that weren't easy to soothe most of the time. But I kept repeating to myself: "She's supposed to cry for three hours a day. This is good for her lungs." Then when she was still sleeping and I just wanted to go do something or get some interaction back, I would remember, "She's supposed to sleep for sixteen hours a day."

This has been a helpful perspective that I've applied to many relationships in my life, not just parenting. To take a step back and be realistic about what others or things are actually able to offer.

REALISTIC WITH HOPE

I am always "glass half full" and "a world full of possibilities" in my approach to life. My husband is always "glass is actually a third of the way full" and "facts are facts, Becky." He can be such a joy-kill to my idealism and big dreams. In reality, he is just the perfect balance to me, and I to him. We need both. Our expectations of the holidays need to be balanced with freedom and discipline.

You have freedom and permission to dream and hope in big things for your holidays. We want to set goals and go after a better way; that's why I've written a chapter for each holiday, so we can walk through each season together. We want to learn from others, taking the good pieces from their holidays and implementing them with ours. We want to go to our Father with open hands and ask what He wants for our holidays, making room for less chaos and more Jesus. Your Father is a creative God who also did things in unexpected ways, oftentimes in a way that seemed impossible. Tap into the same creativity you've inherited in Him and ask Him to do what seems impossible—full of faith in God and grace for yourself and others.

To the same extent you have freedom to dream and hope, make it your goal to also be realistic. Being realistic is not the same thing as being a defeatist, a pessimist, or thinking the world is out to get you. Being realistic means we expect from others, ourselves, and the holidays what they are actually able to give.

We've heard Romans 8:28 before, that "all things work together for good . . ." Certainly out of context this sounds nice, doesn't it? But in context, it sounds even better and really fits in with what we are trying to understand about being realistic while going into the holidays with wide-eyed expectation. Our God can use anything and do anything!

Read Romans 8:18–30 and underline what it teaches you about yourself and God in light of your hopes, realities, and expectations.

For I consider that the sufferings of this present time are not worth comparing with the glory that is to be revealed to us. For the creation waits with eager longing for the revealing of the sons of God. For the creation was subjected to futility, not willingly, but because of him who subjected it, in hope that the creation itself will be set free from its bondage to corruption and obtain the freedom of the glory of the children of God. For we know that the whole creation has been groaning together in the pains of childbirth until now. And not only the creation, but we ourselves, who have the firstfruits of the Spirit, groan inwardly as we wait eagerly for adoption as sons, the redemption of our bodies. For in this hope we were saved. Now hope that is seen is not hope. For who hopes for what he sees? But if we hope for what we do not see, we wait for it with patience.

Likewise the Spirit helps us in our weakness. For we do not know what to pray for as we ought, but the Spirit himself intercedes for us with groanings too deep for words. And he who searches hearts knows what is the mind of the Spirit, because the Spirit intercedes for the saints according to the will of God. And we know that for those who love God all things work together for good, for those who are called according to his purpose. For those whom he foreknew he also predestined to be conformed to the image of his Son, in order that he might be the firstborn among many brothers. And those whom he predestined he also called, and those whom he called he also justified, and those whom he justified he also glorified.

We have to trust that God, who foreknew and predestined us, wants our holidays to honor Him, His Son, and the Spirit. That He is actively working for our good because it brings Him glory. That His Spirit helps us in our weaknesses and will show us how to pray and hope when we feel clueless. Then we live out verse 25 and "wait for it with patience."

GET REAL

When we choose to have realistic expectations for ourselves, others, and the holiday itself, we will find that the holiday will be much more enjoyable . . . for everyone!

Before we can get real with our future expectations, let's get real about our past expectations. What I want us to do next is to quickly evaluate some of the ways you've been unrealistic with the holidays.

Evaluate Your Past Expectations

Take some time to pause and ask yourself these questions about each holiday:

- What hopes have I had for this holiday that is rarely, if ever, met?
- Who are people who fail at meeting my expectations? Why?
- How do I disappoint myself during this holiday?
- What are other unmet expectations for this holiday?

NEW YEAR'S:

_____

_____

VALENTINE'S DAY:

_____

_____

LENT AND EASTER:

_____

_____

SUMMER:

_____

_____

HALLOWEEN:

_____

_____

THANKSGIVING:

_____

_____

ADVENT AND CHRISTMAS:

_____

_____

HAPPY BIRTHDAY (INCLUDING YOUR BIRTHDAY AND OTHERS):

_____

_____

Great work going through that! I hope it provided insight into all the ways you expected more out of a particular holiday, others, or yourself. It's good to look back and learn from the past, but if all we do is look back on the past, we will settle into regret or bitterness.

Let's choose to change our expectations for each of these holidays. Let's approach our expectations with realism mixed with a little excitement over what could be. We can have both.

Set Your Future Expectations

Take some time to pause and ask yourself these questions about each holiday as you set your future expectations, choosing to be realistic while hopeful for good things:

- What hopes do I have for this holiday? Will this take time or can it change instantly?
- Who are people involved in this holiday and what can I expect from them, due to their physical, spiritual, and/or emotional maturity?
- How can I live differently this holiday? What would I like to "be like"? Who do I feel called to be during this holiday?

NEW YEAR'S:

_____

_____

VALENTINE'S DAY:

_____

_____

LENT AND EASTER:

_____

_____

SUMMER:

_____

_____

HALLOWEEN:

_____

_____

THANKSGIVING:

_____

_____

ADVENT AND CHRISTMAS:

_____

_____

**HAPPY BIRTHDAY (INCLUDING YOUR
BIRTHDAY AND OTHERS):**

_____

_____

Setting expectations that are full of hope and are realistic isn't an easy thing to do. I'm really proud of you for doing this! This would be a good page to come back to with each season and update your expectations. As you approach each one with faith, you will see God begin to work! As He works, you will be able to update your expectations.

Don't lose your hope in the reality, and don't let dreams for bigger things keep you from living realistically. This is the tension we live in as followers of Jesus. We know He is more than able as we follow the Spirit's leading.

CHAPTER 13

CONFLICT, DRAMA, AND ALL THE FEELS

The number one struggle I hear from women during the holidays is having to deal with so much conflict or drama. (Money and busyness are close runners-up and will be discussed in the next chapters.)

It doesn't matter which holiday is being celebrated, conflict will inevitably come up. As we discuss the issue of conflict and drama, I want us to look at it from your unique perspective. Obviously, this will change from year to year as past conflicts are resolved and new ones arise. However, let's start off clearly identifying the current issues. Don't skip past this part or sugarcoat things. Be honest and vulnerable, so that things can become healthy. In order to see our holidays become sacred—holy and set apart—we must let the Spirit do a work in all areas.

WHAT ARE CONSISTENT POINTS OF CONFLICT, DRAMA, OR HEAVY FEELINGS?

NEW YEAR'S:

_____

_____

VALENTINE'S DAY:

_____

_____

LENT AND EASTER:

_____

_____

SUMMER:

_____

_____

HALLOWEEN:

_____

_____

THANKSGIVING:

_____

_____

ADVENT AND CHRISTMAS:

_____

_____

**HAPPY BIRTHDAY (INCLUDING YOUR
BIRTHDAY AND OTHERS):**

_____

_____

Just as a doctor doesn't treat only the symptoms, but also needs to know what is at the root or source of the issue, we must get to the root of conflict or drama to clearly identify the best course of action. In looking at your list of potential areas of conflict, I wonder if you are able to identify a thread of consistency. Maybe the majority of your points of conflict have to deal with one person. Maybe there is a consistent root of jealousy throughout.

Whatever your root is, record it below:

If you aren't sure what your root(s) is, take a little bit of time and ask your Father to reveal it to you. Ask Him to show you what is at the root of all the conflict and drama. It is likely multiple things. Being able to pinpoint something like this is huge, because it allows you to generally and then specifically deal with it and take it to the Lord. As we move forward through this chapter, keep that root in mind.

AN EASIER WAY

Before I became a Christian in high school, I remember people would try to convince me that believing in Jesus was the way to go because of the peace I would find in Him. They "sold" it as if following Jesus would make all my troubles fade away, and I would just feel peaceful all the time—life would be easy. Even though that wasn't the reason I chose to follow Him, I felt scammed by those people at the beginning because things did not seem so peaceful. In fact, it seemed like things had gotten a lot more complicated by choosing to follow Jesus. Everything was turned upside down. In time I understood what they were trying to say: Jesus' presence brings peace because He is in control of all things. I came to believe this more as I began to follow Him. As we address conflict and drama in this chapter, I want you to hear the words your Savior spoke in Matthew 11:28–30,

> "Come to me, all who labor and are heavy laden, and I will give you rest. Take my yoke upon you, and learn from me, for I am gentle and lowly in heart, and you will find rest for your souls. For my yoke is easy, and my burden is light."

You weren't meant to suck it up during the holidays or figure it out on your own. Jesus Christ Himself said that He wants us to come to Him with all that we have been carrying around. He says that He will give us rest. Sometimes we do absolutely nothing and just expect, or at least hope, that next year it will be better. Jesus says that we can find rest in Him. Doesn't that sound amazing? He tells us that we will find rest by taking on His yoke. This sounds counterintuitive, doesn't it? Why would we take on more when we already feel overwhelmed? What we take on is His yoke—when we are linked to Him. He reassures us, though, that He is gentle and lowly in heart, and that we will find rest for our souls once we take on His yoke. Then again He reassures us that His yoke, what we need to take up, is easy and the burden is light.

I know many of you hold burdens that feel anything but light. A quick scan of your list of conflicts, while processing through each one, proves that. So instead of carrying those burdens any longer, let's lay them down and pick up His yoke. Let's hear what

He has to say about some key conflict issues, drama roots, and feelings.

EVEN JESUS WAS TEMPTED, FIGHT LIKE HIM

In Matthew 4 we find Jesus being tempted by Satan in the wilderness. We know that Satan is crafty (Gen. 3:1), a liar (actually the father of lies according to John 8:44), and a thief who comes to "steal and kill and destroy" (John 10:10). The way we see Jesus fight Satan is with the Word of God. Each time He shuts the father of lies up with the truth of God, His Word.

The next section is a list of verses to help you when facing some very common points of conflict. Sometimes our tendency can be to skip over or mentally check out when we read Scripture in a book. We got the book to get a person's thoughts on something, and because of that we can skip past Scriptures and quotes. Don't do that this time. I love what Isaiah 55:1–3, 8–13 teaches us about the importance of seeking God and the power of His Word:

> "Come, everyone who thirsts, come to the waters; . . . Why do you spend your money for that which is not bread, and your labor for that which does not satisfy? Listen diligently to me, and eat what is good, and delight yourselves in rich food. Incline your ear, and come to me; hear, that your soul may live; and I will make with you an everlasting covenant. . . . For my thoughts are not your thoughts, neither are your ways my ways, declares the LORD. For as the heavens are higher than the earth, so are my ways higher than your ways and my thoughts than your thoughts.
>
> For as the rain and the snow come down from heaven and do not return there but water the earth, making it bring forth and sprout, giving seed to the sower and bread to the eater, so shall my word be that goes out from my mouth; it shall not return to me empty, but it shall accomplish that which I purpose, and shall succeed in the thing for which I sent it.

For you shall go out in joy and be led forth in peace; the mountains and the hills before you shall break forth into singing, and all the trees of the field shall clap their hands. Instead of the thorn shall come up the cypress; instead of the brier shall come up the myrtle; and it shall make a name for the LORD, an everlasting sign that shall not be cut off."

Yes to all of that! My hope for you in the following sections is that you would go to the Father when you feel dry or empty. That you would go to His Word and listen diligently and consume the goodness of the Bread of Life. That you would stop going to others first to hear or read their thoughts, and instead that you would come to Him and listen. One of the coolest verses comes in verses 8–9 when He tells us that His ways and thoughts are so much higher than anything we could come up with. If that is true, and it is, why do we keep trying to figure this out on our own? He always has a better way! Let's let His Word rain down on our dry land, our hearts, because He says that His Word will not return void but it will do the very thing He sent it out to do! Isn't that amazing? We will be able to go out in joy and be led in peace! His Word turns our conflict and drama into joy and peace! Then verse 13 paints a beautiful picture for us that I hope gives you so much hope. What once was dead or dormant becomes alive and beautiful. Winter, when all the leaves and flowers fade, will soon pass, and spring will come. In time the color will break through and life will burst forth. This is what your Father can do!

Often, as women, we are quick to seek advice from others, or at least vent without any desire to get advice in return. (Tell me I'm right on this.) When something has happened, we instantly reach for our phone to text or call whoever is "our person." What we have become increasingly lazy in doing, myself included, is going to our Father first, to confide in Him first, to seek Him first. This is hard. Because He is an invisible God, we often forget that He is also a present God.

SPECIFIC SCRIPTURES TO DEAL
WITH POINTS OF CONFLICT

Use this next section as a resource. When an issue pops up in one of these areas, flip to the category and let Scripture lead you to what is best. Here are a few things you can do with these verses:

- Let them correct you (we should focus on ourselves first, instead of the other person involved in the conflict).
- Let them direct you to the best way to respond to your situation.
- Use them as a prayer guide; pray these verses over your situation.
- Add more verses in the space provided for each topic that ministers to you.

Conflict with Others

I won't provide much commentary on these areas because I believe His Word more than speaks for itself. However, I want to draw attention to this verse I am about to share. I believe that if we, as followers of Christ, handled conflict first according to this process, so many of our issues would be nonexistent or quickly resolved. We escalate them by all of our "seeking wise counsel" and avoiding conflict for the sake of "turning the other cheek." Or sometimes it's because dealing with conflict feels contrary to the peace and forgiveness that we think we should feel as Christians. Avoidance is not the same thing as peace. As you already know, it only festers, and festering isn't very pretty.

> "If your brother sins against you, go and tell him his fault, between you and him alone. If he listens to you, you have gained your brother. But if he does not listen, take one or two others along with you, that every charge may be established by the evidence of two or three witnesses. If he refuses to listen to them, tell it to the church. And if he

refuses to listen even to the church, let him be to you as a Gentile and a tax collector." (Matt. 18:15–17)

Jesus answered, "The most important is, 'Hear, O Israel: The Lord our God, the Lord is one. And you shall love the Lord your God with all your heart and with all your soul and with all your mind and with all your strength.' The second is this: 'You shall love your neighbor as yourself.' There is no other commandment greater than these." (Mark 12:29–31)

One thing I was taught many years ago is that if we are called to love then we should define love with the way we live. First Corinthians 13 gives us great definitions for love. As you pray this verse over yourself, replace the word "love" (or "it") with your name. With each characteristic, ask your Father to help you become that.

Love is patient and kind; love does not envy or boast; it is not arrogant or rude. It does not insist on its own way; it is not irritable or resentful; it does not rejoice at wrongdoing, but rejoices with the truth. Love bears all things, believes all things, hopes all things, endures all things. (1 Cor. 13:4–7)

"The thief comes only to steal and kill and destroy. I came that they may have life and have it abundantly." (John 10:10)

"Judge not, and you will not be judged; condemn not, and you will not be condemned; forgive, and you will be forgiven; give, and it will be given to you. Good measure, pressed down, shaken together, running over, will be put into your lap. For with the measure you use it will be measured back to you." (Luke 6:37–38)

If possible, so far as it depends on you, live peaceably with all. Beloved, never avenge yourselves, but leave it to the wrath of God, for it is written, "Vengeance is mine, I will repay, says the Lord." (Rom. 12:18–19)

Do nothing from selfish ambition or conceit, but in humility count others more significant than yourselves. Let each of you look not only to his own interests, but also to the interests of others. (Phil. 2:3–4)

Put on then, as God's chosen ones, holy and beloved, compassionate hearts, kindness, humility, meekness, and patience, bearing with one another and, if one has a complaint against another, forgiving each other; as the Lord has forgiven you, so you also must forgive. And above all these put on love, which binds everything together in perfect harmony. (Col. 3:12–14)

Record other verses or advice about conflict with others for your reference over the years to come:

Bitterness and Anger

"The LORD will fight for you, and you have only to be silent." (Exod. 14:14)

A soft answer turns away wrath, but a harsh word stirs up anger. (Prov. 15:1)

Good sense makes one slow to anger, and it is his glory to overlook an offense. (Prov. 19:11)

"You have heard that it was said, 'An eye for an eye and a tooth for a tooth.' But I say to you, Do not resist the one who is evil. But if anyone slaps you on the right cheek, turn to him the other also. And if anyone would sue you and take your tunic, let him have your cloak as well. And if anyone forces you to go one mile, go with him two miles. Give to the one who begs from you, and do not refuse the one who would borrow from you." (Matt. 5:38–42)

Be angry and do not sin; do not let the sun go down on your anger. (Eph. 4:26)

Let no corrupting talk come out of your mouths, but only such as is good for building up, as fits the occasion, that it may give grace to those who hear. (Eph. 4:29)

Strive for peace with everyone, and for the holiness without which no one will see the Lord. See to it that no one fails to obtain the grace of God; that no "root of bitterness" springs up and causes trouble, and by it many become defiled. (Heb. 12:14–15)

Know this, my beloved brothers: let every person be quick to hear, slow to speak, slow to anger; for the anger of man does not produce the righteousness of God. (James 1:19–20)

Finally, all of you, have unity of mind, sympathy, brotherly love, a tender heart, and a humble mind. Do not repay evil for evil or reviling for reviling, but on the contrary, bless, for to this you were called, that you may obtain a blessing. (1 Pet. 3:8–9)

Record other verses or advice about bitterness and anger for your reference over the years to come:

Unforgiveness

"So if you are offering your gift at the altar and there remember that your brother has something against you, leave your gift there before the altar and go. First be reconciled to your brother, and then come and offer your gift." (Matt. 5:23–24)

"And forgive us our debts, as we also have forgiven our debtors." (Matt. 6:12)

"And whenever you stand praying, forgive, if you have anything against anyone, so that your Father also who is in heaven may forgive you your trespasses." (Mark 11:25)

"Pay attention to yourselves! If your brother sins, rebuke him, and if he repents, forgive him, and if he sins against you seven times in the day, and turns to you seven times, saying, 'I repent,' you must forgive him." (Luke 17:3–4)

Be kind to one another, tenderhearted, forgiving one another, as God in Christ forgave you. (Eph. 4:32)

If anyone says, "I love God," and hates his brother, he is a liar; for he who does not love his brother whom he has seen cannot love God whom he has not seen. And this commandment we have from him: whoever loves God must also love his brother. (1 John 4:20–21)

Record other verses or advice about unforgiveness for your refer-ence over the years to come:

Stress and Being Overwhelmed

Cast your burden on the LORD and he will sustain you; he will never permit the righteous to be moved. (Ps. 55:22)

Out of my distress I called on the LORD; the LORD answered me and set me free. The LORD is on my side; I will not fear. What can man do to me? The LORD is on my side as my helper. (Ps. 118:5–7)

Trust in the LORD with all your heart, and do not lean on your own understanding. In all your ways acknowledge him, and he will make straight your paths. (Prov. 3:5–6)

For I know the plans I have for you, declares the LORD, plans for welfare and not for evil, to give you a future and a hope. Then you will call upon me and come and pray to me, and I will hear you. You will seek me and find me, when you seek me with all your heart. (Jer. 29:11–13)

"But seek first the kingdom of God and his righteous-ness, and all these things will be added to you. Therefore do not be anxious about tomorrow, for tomorrow will be anxious for itself. Sufficient for the day is its own trouble." (Matt. 6:33–34)

"But the Helper, the Holy Spirit, whom the Father will send in my name, he will teach you all things and bring to your remembrance all that I have said to you. Peace I leave with you; my peace I give to you. Not as the world gives do I give to you. Let not your hearts be troubled, neither let them be afraid." (John 14:26–27)

"I have said these things to you, that in me you may have peace. In the world you will have tribulation. But take heart; I have overcome the world." (John 16:33)

And we know that for those who love God all things work together for good, for those who are called according to his purpose. (Rom. 8:28)

Casting all your anxieties on him, because he cares for you. Be sober-minded; be watchful. Your adversary the devil prowls around like a roaring lion, seeking someone to devour. Resist him, firm in your faith, knowing that the same kinds of suffering are being experienced by your brotherhood throughout the world. (1 Pet. 5:7–9)

Record other verses or advice about stress and being overwhelmed for your reference over the years to come:

Loneliness

"It is the LORD who goes before you. He will be with you; he will not leave you or forsake you. Do not fear or be dismayed." (Deut. 31:8)

"Be strong and courageous. Do not be frightened, and do not be dismayed, for the LORD your God is with you wherever you go." (Josh. 1:9)

Even though I walk through the valley of the shadow of death, I will fear no evil, for you are with me; your rod and your staff, they comfort me. (Ps. 23:4)

Turn to me and be gracious to me, for I am lonely and afflicted. (Ps. 25:16)

God is our refuge and strength, a very present help in trouble. (Ps. 46:1)

He who dwells in the shelter of the Most High will abide in the shadow of the Almighty. I will say to the Lord, "My refuge and my fortress, my God, in whom I trust." (Ps. 91:1–2)

The Lord is near to all who call on him, to all who call on him in truth. (Ps. 145:18)

"Fear not, for I am with you; be not dismayed, for I am your God; I will strengthen you, I will help you, I will uphold you with my righteous right hand." (Isa. 41:10)

"When you pass through the waters, I will be with you; and through the rivers, they shall not overwhelm you; when you walk through fire you shall not be burned, and the flame shall not consume you." (Isa. 43:2)

By this we know that we abide in him and he in us, because he has given us of his Spirit. (1 John 4:13)

Record other verses or advice about loneliness for your reference over the years to come:

COUNT IT ALL JOY

Since high school I've dealt with a chronic health issue. It's one of those things that others would have no clue about. It's nothing too serious, but it will never go away. I've had twelve surgeries for it over the years and had countless doctors promise to be the one to find a cure for this, and no one has. It has been a frustrating rollercoaster. Likely, you have a rollercoaster of your own of ups and downs and you just don't know when it will end. When I'm on the coaster and it's ticking to the top and I know that big drop is coming, one of my favorite verses to read is James 1:2–4, "Count it all joy, my brothers, when you meet trials of various kinds, for you know that the testing of your faith produces steadfastness. And let steadfastness have its full effect, that you may be perfect and complete, lacking in nothing."

Most of us have experienced the pain of trials and the testing of our faith. We also know how much stronger they make us. I wish there was another way, and I could remove the struggle of it. However, His Word tells us the struggle is what is giving us strength, making us perfect and whole. Isn't that strange? In times of struggle we often pray for God to provide another way, a way out of the conflict and struggle. But what if this struggle was His provision? Hear me: if trials and testing of our faith bring about steadfastness, and steadfastness will eventually have the effect of us being "perfect and complete, lacking in nothing"; if we didn't walk through the trial, then we could never be whole. So the thing that makes us fully ourselves isn't great advice from others, or stuffing down or ignoring conflict and pain, nor is it trying to fix the solution. The thing that makes us whole and perfect is being steadfast—immovable, not subject to change, firm in belief— through the trial.

We've all known that person, or maybe we are that person, who is so much stronger because of what we've walked through. It is one of the things I pray often for myself as I parent my girls: as much as I want to protect them, I don't want to shelter them from trials. I have learned personally, through countless trials, that they make me stronger. I may feel like I'm not going to survive some of them, that there's no light at the end of the tunnel. But He is the light, and His Word lights our path (Ps. 119:105).

So let's live out James 1:22, "But be doers of the word, and not hearers only, deceiving yourselves." Let's go to His Word in the midst of our conflict and drama and do what it says!

| CHAPTER 14 |

BUDGETS AND GENEROSITY

I was joking today with my husband, Chris, about how I think he should guest or ghostwrite this chapter. Well, I half-joked, because if he had taken me up on it, I would've let him!

I know this chapter goes in this book because we all need to hear what's in it. But I just want to say upfront that I don't like this chapter at all. So for those of you reading this who have an allergy to budgets, in solidarity let's keep going with this chapter because we need it. I told Chris, "Well, they say that those who can't do, teach. So I'll just teach this, even though I can't do it very well." Then he said what he always says when I, or one of our girls, use the *can't* word, "Becky, take the *t* out of can't." It makes me roll my eyes every single time he says it, but, irritatingly enough, it's true.

We all approach money differently, but most of us gravitate toward a certain end of the spectrum—we either extremely control or extremely spend. My hope for each of us is to find some emotional freedom and grace, get some practical tips to help make the holidays more smooth, and create space to be more generous. How does that sound? You can do it, both my budget-freak friends and my shopaholic friends.

STRESS AND GRACE

We have a built-in intuition about money, don't we? We know what we should do and we know what we feel better doing. We know we feel stressed when we don't have money. We know we feel guilty when we spend too much money. And we typically wish we had more money. Most of us, I believe, want to be generous with others during the holidays. And Target doesn't make it any easier on us to *not* go crazy during each and every holiday, with their perfectly displayed items that we can't go home without.

So why do finances cause us so much stress? The answer is twofold: we are poor stewards of our finances and we don't trust that what God's given us is enough.

The first one is entirely on us and I don't say that to shame you; I say that to correct us. Our being stressed has very little to do with not actually having enough money, but everything to do with not being very good stewards of what we have. I see this becoming increasingly more prevalent with each generation. Perhaps the culprit is the rise of media and then social media, making us believe we should have all the things without learning the value of waiting. So instead, we charge or overspend because we want it now and feel like we deserve it now. This is on us and it's something we must take before the Lord in repentance.

Do you need to repent of poor spending habits or poor attitude toward money? If so, do that now. Do not wait.

The second issue is less a sin issue and more a trust issue: we don't trust that what God has given is enough. Jesus addresses this in Matthew 6:25–34:

"Therefore I tell you, do not be anxious about your life, what you will eat or what you will drink, nor about your body, what you will put on. Is not life more than food, and the body more than clothing? Look at the birds of the air: they neither sow nor reap nor gather into barns, and yet your heavenly Father feeds them. Are you not of more value than they? And which of you by being anxious can add a single hour to his span of life? And why are you anxious about clothing? Consider the lilies of the field, how they grow: they neither toil nor spin, yet I tell you, even Solomon in all his glory was not arrayed like one of these. But if God so clothes the grass of the field, which today is alive and tomorrow is thrown into the oven, will he not much more clothe you, O you of little faith? Therefore do not be anxious, saying, 'What shall we eat?' or 'What shall we drink?' or 'What shall we wear?' For the Gentiles seek after all these things, and your heavenly Father knows that you need them all. But seek first the kingdom of God and his righteousness, and all these things will be added to you. Therefore do not be anxious about tomorrow, for tomorrow will be anxious for itself. Sufficient for the day is its own trouble."

What great comfort, right? If God takes care of the flowers and the birds, He can easily provide for you. The real issue comes down to not just trusting that He will provide but believing that His provision is *best*. Oftentimes the Lord has provided and has said yes, but it just doesn't look the way we would choose.

This might be a good time to stop and pray and ask the Lord to give you both trust that He will provide and belief that His provision is best.

SOME HELPFUL TIPS

Now that we have dealt with our hearts, let's talk about some practical tips that work. I half joked at the beginning of the chapter that finances are something I struggle with doing well. The truth is that it gets better and better each year, and not because our income has so drastically increased. Since we make it a point to learn more each year, we improve more each year—never perfect but always improving. Here are a few tips we've implemented, along with a few I've recently learned from friends.

Make Other Sacrifices throughout the Year

This is the one no one likes. The truth is, your budget is what it is, and we can wish for more money all day long, but the way you create more money now is to spend less. For some, that seems impossible to do. For many of us, though, we can find places to cut down—or cut entirely—to create space in our budgets.

Look at your past three months of spending and ask yourself about each item, "Was this really needed?" Look at your past few trips to the grocery store or Target, and ask yourself, "Did I really need this?" Look at your credit card statement and ask yourself the same question. Most of us will be able to find some money to set aside in order to buy gifts for others.

The fun, or rather meaningful, part about this is when we choose to stop spending in order to save, the items we purchase later with our saved money will feel less like a sacrifice. For example, you may pick up a fancy latte on the way to work, but those little expenses add up. So you choose to only drink coffee at home, saving the money you would typically spend at the coffee shop. Say you spend $30 on lattes each month but decide to cut that down to a once-a-month treat; now you are saving $25 a month. Which is $300 a year—a great gift and celebration budget!

Budget for Gifts All Year Long

This has, by far, been the best tip when it comes to budgets and our ability to be generous! We list all the things we want to purchase for each of the holidays, and then divide that number by twelve, putting that amount aside each month into a separate category. This has removed all guilt and shame that used to cloud my joy in giving and celebrating others. I no longer feel those negative emotions because the money is already there.

The next section of this chapter allows you to really break that down. Give yourself time to do this, even if you don't have all the numbers together right now. Like the rest of this book, use this as a resource that you come back to again and again.

Use Cash or Gift Cards

Maybe you aren't the budgeting or planning-in-advance type, yet you don't like the idea of overspending or going into debt when celebrating others. A great tip is to use a cash system when it comes to shopping. So if you want to buy some gifts that month, at the beginning of the month, pull that amount out of your checking account.

Another tip a friend has shared is to buy yourself gift cards all throughout the year to the stores where you love buying gifts. Then when it's time to buy someone a gift, you don't have to stress about having money—it's already taken care of with gift cards!

Buy All Year Long and During Peak Sales

This takes some planning, but it can be done and is a great way to take advantage of sales all year long. I keep a running list on my phone of people I like to buy gifts for, then I stay on the lookout. I know some friends who buy all-year-round for birthday gifts or Christmas, even if it is a year away. Personally, I can't plan things out that far in advance, but I am learning that giving myself a little more time helps me take advantage of sales.

Thoughtfulness over Quantity

I know the saying typically goes "quality over quantity," but I think we still have it wrong with that mantra. It's true that we need less stuff. I mean, do we ever need more stuff? But we've taken "quality" to mean that we should instead give something really nice—but that's not the solution either.

We've all been given gift cards and we loved them. But when you think of the most treasured gifts you've been given, have you ever once thought about a gift card? Likely no, unless it had some real thoughtfulness attached to it.

One huge way you can bring a lot more meaning to your holidays is to give more meaningful gifts. These meaningful gifts don't always have a price tag, or a very high one. One of the most meaningful gifts Chris and I have given one another is a stack of Post-its for Christmas. This is something we've each done a couple of times now, and it's the most favorite gift we've given each other to date and it cost us less than $5. That stack of Post-its sat on our bathroom counter for an entire year, and each day we would write one thing we loved about each other or were grateful for one another.

Challenge yourself, especially if your budget is tight or non-existent, to find ways to be more thoughtful. It requires a little more time in prep, but I can promise you will have a lot more fun being generous and your loved ones will enjoy their gifts even more!

BREAKING THE BUDGET DOWN

I am about to ask you to do something that might be a little sobering. We love to be generous, and if we could give everyone a gift and throw them a party, I think most of us would. However, costs add up. Quickly. I want to help you see what things can add up to. You will have to use estimates here, but do your best to be accurate.

*List Your Expenses for Each Holiday and Then
Find the Total*

Here are some questions you can ask yourself for each holiday:

- Who would you like to buy gifts for? List each person and amount per person.
- How much will you spend on packaging and shipping?
- Would you like to buy decor? How much would you spend on decor?
- Would you like to be able to celebrate with dinner or a party? How much?

NEW YEAR'S: (TOTAL BUDGET: $_____)

_____

_____

VALENTINE'S DAY: (TOTAL BUDGET: $_____)

_____

_____

LENT AND EASTER: (TOTAL BUDGET: $_____)

_____

_____

SUMMER: (TOTAL BUDGET: $_____)

_____

_____

HALLOWEEN: (TOTAL BUDGET: $_____)

_____

_____

THANKSGIVING: (TOTAL BUDGET: $_____)

_____

_____

ADVENT AND CHRISTMAS: (TOTAL BUDGET: $_____)

_____

_____

HAPPY BIRTHDAY (INCLUDING YOUR BIRTHDAY AND OTHERS): (TOTAL BUDGET: $_____)

_____

_____

Now Add Up All Your Totals and Fill in the Space Below:

TOTAL TO SPEND FOR
ALL HOLIDAYS: $_____

This is the number you need to have saved so that you can remove the stress of finances from your plate. As I said before, we took this number and divided it by twelve. As we've gotten raises or a bonus, we've been able to increase the budget. What we don't do is allow ourselves to go over it by too much, as much as my Target- and Amazon Prime-loving self would like to.

The truth is, all of these things are extras. I need to hear that as much as the next person. We don't need more holiday decor, even if it was on sale. We don't need to get that person just one more gift (or even the one gift). I don't believe anyone on your gift list would rather you go over budget, into debt, or feel stress because you wanted to get them an awesome gift, pick up the tab at a meal, or throw a fun gathering.

TWO OF OUR FAVORITE RESOURCES

There are two resources that have completely reshaped our finances, and my very immature emotional approach to it. I wanted to share these as recommendations for you.

Dave Ramsey and Financial Peace University

Dave Ramsey has become a bit of a household curse word. I'm teasing . . . sort of.

He has the Financial Peace University course that helps you "live like no one else, so you can live like no one else." The course is all about getting out of debt quickly, living on what you actually have, and being generous.

Let me tell you something: it's not very fun at the beginning. To live like no one else means saying *no* a lot. I hated this . . . I still hate this. I would often say to Chris, "I don't understand why we can't do X and all of our friends are doing X!" As Theodore Roosevelt said, "Comparison is the thief of joy." It was ten years ago when I was feeling really sad for myself for not being able to do the things our friends were doing. Now, while we still have a long way to go, we're seeing the light at the end of the tunnel of the second part of "living like no one else." I don't share this to brag, because we have certainly not made it yet, but to encourage you: you will get there! Slow and steady wins the race.

I wish I had started this before I even went to college and then did a refresher on it every year after that. One thing I love about Dave, in his courses, is that he reassures you that now is a better time to start than later. He encourages you to start living this way today, which is the soonest opportunity you have now. He also shows you that if you start today, even if you are in your fifties or older, it will still benefit you. Don't let fear or age, young or old, keep you from making a financial plan.

*You can learn more at daveramsey.com
or by following @daveramsey.*

You Need a Budget (YNAB): Tools and Tracking

Full disclosure: I do not use YNAB computer software, but Chris uses it faithfully because he really loves tracking. I do reference it when we have our budget meetings. Here is what I love about YNAB: it's really user-friendly, even I can input things and find categories easily (this is saying a lot). They also provide some really great tips and resources to help you in budgeting and tracking.

*You can learn more at youneedabudget.com
or by following @youneedabudget.*

GENEROSITY

We really can't begin to talk about being truly generous until we truly get our finances in order. I have learned this lesson the hard way. Once we get our finances in place, we are freed up to be generous—with our money, time, and heart.

The final tip that I can offer you in this financial chapter is sharing your goal to be generous. I want you to dream bigger than you've ever dreamed before when it comes to being generous. Pray through each holiday and ask the Lord to show you ways you could be generous.

Generosity Dream List

NEW YEAR'S:

_____

_____

VALENTINE'S DAY:

_____

_____

LENT AND EASTER:

_____

_____

SUMMER:

_____

_____

HALLOWEEN:

_____

_____

THANKSGIVING:

_____

_____

ADVENT AND CHRISTMAS:

_____

_____

**HAPPY BIRTHDAY (INCLUDING YOUR
BIRTHDAY AND OTHERS):**

_____

_____

Generosity is the goal and can sometimes explain why we struggle with overspending at the holidays. We want to make others feel loved and special, so we buy them things and try to make the day or season as memorable as possible. Your heart in this isn't ugly; it's actually quite beautiful. However, giving certain gifts, decorating like crazy, or picking up the tab for the celebration just isn't worth putting yourself in a bad financial place. You will likely have to be a little more creative, but that can also be a lot of fun and will be a really cute story for years to come!

CHAPTER 15

SCHEDULES AND PLANS

I don't watch a lot of TV, but I am pretty loyal to the Pearson family from *This Is Us*. One of my favorite episodes in season one is when they chose to redefine Thanksgiving. Rebecca, the mom, was stressed. Everyone was dressed up in clothes they didn't like, loading up for a car ride they didn't want to take. Then their car broke down, and they had to walk miles to make it to this shady motel where they ate gas station food—and they absolutely loved it. After that, they decided it was the best Thanksgiving ever and decided to do Thanksgiving that way for all future years.

They chose that year to make new traditions, ones that brought them joy and true connectivity. This is my hope for myself, my family, and it's my greatest hope for you with this chapter.

I know that adulthood is hard, and holidays as an adult can be *really* hard. It's hard if you are single, it's hard if you are married, it's hard if you have children, it's hard if you are divorced, and it's hard if you are widowed. It's hard if you are wealthy; it's hard if you are poor. It's hard if you like your family, it's hard if you don't like your family, and it's hard if you have no family at all. Holidays are hard, but we have the choice to seek out joy and meaning.

Next to unmet expectations and financial stressors, we are often pulled between multiple people or places during the holidays, where hectic schedules don't bring very much joy.

JUST SAY NO AND SET BOUNDARIES

I want you to try something with me. Say no. Yes, out loud and right now. I don't care how silly you feel, say out loud the word *no*. It's possible.

This has been one of the hardest parts about becoming an adult is telling the other adults in my life no. *No, I will not come. No, I will not stay that long. No, I can't afford that. No, I don't find that funny.* No. It has led to a lot of hard conversations and some tears, from myself and them. Saying no isn't an easy thing to do, but it is a very healthy thing to do.

Oftentimes, as followers of Jesus, we feel like we should say yes to everyone, especially family. Aren't we supposed to love others? How is saying no loving them well? It's loving them well if saying yes isn't the best choice.

Aren't we supposed to obey our father and our mother? No, not anymore. Ephesians 6:1 does say, "Children, obey your parents in the Lord, for this is right." But you, adult, are no longer a child. You no longer have to obey your parents. You should, however, still aim to honor your parents as Exodus 20:12 says in one of the Ten Commandments, "Honor your father and your mother." Honor does not mean to do whatever that person thinks you should do. Honor is another way to say, "respect them." We can honor our parents and our elders, and still disagree or make a different choice than what they believe to be best.

This is one of the hardest parts about becoming an adult. You will disappoint others, but disappointing others is not the same thing as disrespecting others.

Setting healthy boundaries goes hand-in-hand with saying no. Sometimes saying no is the best way you can set a boundary.

However, sometimes setting healthy boundaries just means you say yes differently.

WEEKLY/MONTHLY/YEARLY SYNC-UP

Much like you, my schedule is complicated during the holidays. Chris and I are both from divorced families, we have three kids, and we both work. Regardless of which stage of life you are in, I highly recommend doing a weekly, monthly, and annual calendar sync-up.

This is where you pull up your calendar and sit down to go over everything. If you have others living with you, I'd recommend involving them in the planning process so you are all on the same page. Sitting down to go over your schedule provides a good overview. You are more able to catch things that you had forgotten to mark down. And you adequately prepare for what is to come. You get to choose what you value and set the standards for what you put on your calendar.

You may need to pick and choose things that you love, so you can do other things you love. For example, I love to speak at women's events and churches. Traveling to see the body of Christ all over the world and teach them from the Word of God is one of my favorite things to do. However, I really love my family and like to spend time with them. So, in some seasons, we have set the standard that I will not commit to traveling more than two times a month. I've had to say no to speaking opportunities if they break this rule, even if I really wanted to say yes.

One problem we face during our sync-up time is the amount of invitations to parties and events that come our way, especially during Christmas time—and we get a lot of invites. The rule at the children's school is you can only send invitations at school if you send one to every kid in the class. And since we have three children, sometimes we're looking at thirty birthday party invitations a year, give or take. That's crazy. It also doesn't even include the things Chris and I are invited to individually or the things we are invited to as a family. So when we get birthday party invitations in the school folder, we talk through with our kids that if they say yes to this one, they will have to say no to another. This practice helps them understand that we can't go to every single party.

I share these examples because you get to choose what you say yes to on your calendar. Our family values time together, so we limit our "yes" to one commitment per weekend.

STOP SAYING YOU ARE SO BUSY

We all act like we are victims of our schedule. I feel like anytime you ask someone how they are doing, their initial response is that they've been really busy. We have overused this word. Our calendars are tools we use, not burdens that we are forced to carry. So if you feel like you are too busy, then do something about it. Use some of the strategies we already discussed and say no; set some boundaries until you no longer feel too busy.

COMMUNICATE CLEARLY AND EARLY

In our day and age, it has never been easier to communicate with others; however, it seems we are losing the art of communication. We no longer know how to communicate the hard things, so we avoid. Listen to me: you need to communicate your expectations and your plans as clearly as you can and as soon as you can.

As you begin to say no and set healthy boundaries, choosing to fill your calendar with the things you believe are best, then you will be forced to have some hard conversations. The sooner you can communicate this with everyone involved, the better for them and for you.

With all that said, let me also say this: You cannot expect an immature person to have a mature conversation. While this doesn't exempt you from making the mature decision to talk to them, you can have realistic expectations about how they might respond. We all have certain people in our lives who make communication a challenge. While you still need to do your part in communicating, we can have realistic expectations for their particular persona. This is a concept that my counselor helped me to understand and it has been a game changer. So if you can get it from this chapter, then I've saved you hundreds of dollars in counseling! Seriously though, know that when you are about to have a conversation with someone, it may not be received well. Take a deep breath, pray, maybe make some notes so you stick to what is best, and have the conversation.

SILVER AND GOLD

My hope is that you can choose and create the holidays you want. You are an adult and actually do have a say in how you want to live your life. Like starting anything new, there will be some aches and pains, but the payoff will be worth it.

There is an old song we used to sing in Girl Scouts, "Make new friends, but keep the old. One is silver and the other is gold." This is how I try to hold holiday schedules and plans—knowing that one is silver and the other is gold. Choosing something new doesn't mean the old is bad; it's simply adding something new to what is good. (On the flip side, there are some traditions that are neither silver or gold; they are coal. We need to toss those completely aside.)

What Are Some Silver and Gold, New and Old, Dreams or Things That You Plan or Want to Do During Each Holiday?

NEW YEAR'S:

_____

_____

VALENTINE'S DAY:

_____

_____

LENT AND EASTER:

_____

_____

SUMMER:

_____

_____

HALLOWEEN:

_____

_____

THANKSGIVING:

_____

_____

ADVENT AND CHRISTMAS:

_____

_____

HAPPY BIRTHDAY (INCLUDING YOUR BIRTHDAY AND OTHERS):

_____

_____

Stick to these silver and gold dreams when you lay out your schedule. Be courageous and loving as you set boundaries that will allow your dreams to have space to evolve. Make time weekly, monthly, and annually to pull out your calendar and make sure you are staying on track with the goals you have. Remember that, as you look at your plans, you are not a slave to your busy schedule; you have all the power. Finally, as you make these changes, communicate your choices as clearly and early as you can.

CHAPTER 16

GRIEF

First, let me tell you that I am so sorry. I wish this wasn't a chapter you felt drawn to read. I wish we could do this over coffee, snuggled up on the couch in my living room. I would make you a steamy cup of some flavored coffee with flavored coffee creamer, unless you are a tea girl; then I'd pull out my box of assorted teas. I would also pull down the treat bin full of chocolate and other goodies because no one cares about all-natural or calories when you just feel sad. Plus, chocolate is kinda organic, so we will just go with that. We would grab a cozy throw and sit on the same couch. I'd take a deep breath and grab your hand and before you even started speaking we would probably both have tears streaming down our faces because this is what girlfriends do. While we can't do this today, know that is my hope and heart with this chapter—that although I'm the one talking, you'll feel heard and understood. I also hope that you hear something that encourages you and gives you some insight on the best next steps for you.

WHEN IT'S NOT SO JOYFUL

Everyone else seems to be having the best season of their life and you want to join the fun, but you just can't. All you notice is that empty chair, your empty arms, or how this day looks nothing like it did in years past. Grief comes in all forms—death, divorce, loss of relationships, infertility, loneliness, sickness, and a myriad of other things. Sometimes the grief is so small or seemingly insignificant we don't even give it the label of grief because we think we should get over it already.

Unfortunately, I think grief can be even harder for believers. Yes, we have so much more comfort in our grief, but we also can have a harder time giving ourselves permission to feel our grief. We feel like we should be better than we are, after all, isn't Jesus our great Comforter (2 Cor. 1:3–5)? We feel shame if we need to get help, because we know that Isaiah 9:6 says that God is our "Wonderful Counselor." So why do we feel so lost or in need of therapy?

Not to mention, when you look around many Christian contexts, everyone else seems to have it all together. I often joke that women know how to put on their "praise Jesus" smiles, raise up their "Glory to God" hands, with their "I'm blessed" responses. So you infer that you must be the only one dealing with something hard. In your head you think that can't be true, but insecurity is a mean bully and it likes to keep us feeling alone.

LONELINESS AND THE LIES SINCE THE BEGINNING OF TIME

We started off alone—Adam was all alone in the garden until the Lord said, "It is not good that the man should be alone; I will make him a helper fit for him" (Gen. 2:18). The world was perfect; there was no grief, pain, sin, or shame; and God was with man in every moment. And even then it wasn't good for man to be alone. We need one another, but the lie is: we don't.

In Genesis 3 we see the serpent, who is Satan, enter the picture. It is said that he was "more crafty than any other beast." John 8:44 says that he is a "liar and the father of lies." In Genesis 2, God's rule for mankind is that they could eat of every single tree in the garden, "but of the tree of the knowledge of good and evil you shall not eat, for in the day that you eat of it you shall surely die."

The first thing Satan, in the form of a serpent, did to Eve was to mess with her mind by asking, "Did God actually say . . . ?" Isn't that just like him? He is always messing with our heads, causing us to question God's words. Then he began to tempt Eve to forget what was true. He questioned her and it worked.

When it comes to grief and being a believer, we can forget what is true, push the pain down, or try to push through, and this is simply not the best thing to do. Like Eve, we can allow the enemy to reshape our view of God and His truth over our lives in the middle of confusing emotions. My hope is that this chapter gives you some encouragement, freedom, and tools to face whatever grief you are in now or in the future. First Peter 5:8 says, "Be sober-minded; be watchful. Your adversary the devil prowls around like a roaring lion, seeking someone to devour."

There's a scene in *Father of the Bride* where Annie has just had a big blowup with her fiancé over being given a 1950s housewife gift. Her dad takes this pitiful groom for drinks and tells him, "We come from a long, long line of over-reactors." He then goes through all the people in his daughter's line who were over-reactors. Chris and I always laugh about this scene and quote it often because our poor girls have inherited the dramatic gene . . . big-time. It is both comical and frustrating to watch it play out. Now that my oldest can really talk through these issues and has recently proclaimed she believes in Jesus, we talk about the spiritual aspects to our feelings. Our feelings are always real and justified, and I always want my kids to be heard. With that said, I also want to raise my girls up to be quick identifiers of lies. We've talked through this story about Eve many times and talk about how there is an enemy who slithers up next to us and whispers lies to us, too. To be able to best deal with our emotions, we must first identify what is true and what is not true.

I hate that in your grief you have to work hard. I wish we could just stay put on my couch talking it through, but the enemy is prowling around like a lion and slithering around like a snake, and he would love nothing more than to whisper crafty and deceiving lies into your ears to keep this season from being sacred—holy and set apart. Instead he would rather this day be closed off from the Father and others. He'd rather you walk around like a robot, just pushing through with your "I'm blessed" retorts with convincing praise hands raised. Let's not give him this win. John 10:10 says, "The thief comes only to steal and kill and destroy. I came that they may have life and have it abundantly."

Let's not let anything else be lost. Let's "be watchful" like 1 Peter 5:8 encourages us, and instead live abundantly, like Jesus said He wants for us in John 10:10.

IT'S OKAY TO NOT BE OKAY . . .
AND OKAY TO BE OKAY

The number one thing I want to tell you is that it's okay to not be okay. Don't stuff your grief down. Instead, feel it. Give yourself permission to feel it. It doesn't matter how many years have passed, grief has no tact and will show up at the most inopportune times. Give those around you a heads-up that you may not be okay. If you know you won't be in your personal surroundings, prepare beforehand how you might handle certain situations that are common triggers for grief. But remember, whether you feel equipped to handle it when it comes and goes—or when it stays—give yourself permission to feel it.

It's also okay to be okay. There might be times you catch yourself laughing or enjoying the holiday, and then you remember. Waves of grief and also guilt overwhelm you. The sadness came back and with it came shame because you were enjoying yourself. As much as you give yourself permission to not be okay, know that it is also okay to be okay. The grief will be back, this we know. So soak up the moments that have made room for joy, even if just for a moment.

KEEP THINGS THE SAME OR CHANGE THEM COMPLETELY

You have permission to do whatever you need to do, and freedom to hop between any of these options throughout the day or season.

Many find great comfort in keeping things as similar as possible, doing things the way they were done before whatever caused the grief. Obviously, something has happened and changed, so it will be different. But many find great comfort in doing many of the things that used to bring joy. Another solution could be to change it up entirely—new plan, new traditions, new settings, etc. Sometimes there is great comfort in celebrations looking nothing like they did in the past. Finally, you can cancel the holiday completely for the first year when the grief is just too strong. Obviously, you won't be able to escape it, but there is nothing wrong with skipping on the celebratory parts of it this year, if you feel you need to. Find what works best for you and give yourself freedom to be flexible.

ASK FOR AND RECEIVE HELP

Sometimes women can be excellent at helping others but terrible at asking for help themselves. Just last week I experienced the reality of this. It was my middle daughter's fifth birthday, and you already know I love to do up birthdays big. However, I came down with the flu and my dad had heart surgery that day. The flu progressed quickly and I was completely out by noon. And my dad's surgery ended up becoming a very serious procedure and they weren't sure he would survive it. It's been a long time since I've felt so helpless. I was stuck in bed while my dad was fighting for his life in the hospital and my husband was making it a fun day for my daughter. Friends were texting and asking what they could do. And finally I said I needed help. I admitted I couldn't do it. I needed prayers and support for my dad. And my family needed good meals, because Chris was juggling a lot taking care of the girls and me. Within an hour my brother booked a flight from NYC to be with my dad and stepmom, since the hospital wouldn't allow me to be there (nor could I pull myself out of bed). And my mom came to take care of me, while some dear friends dropped off meals.

We don't ever want to put others out, but just as it isn't putting you out when they ask for your help, it is a blessing to them when you allow them to help. So whether it's a roommate, spouse, friend, family member, coworker, or neighbor, ask them for help. Invite them into your grief. Let them help in tangible ways. Let them be shoulders to cry on or a listening ear.

COUNSELING IS AWESOME

Getting help from others is wildly important, but sometimes we need a professional's help. There is absolutely no shame in going to a counselor or psychologist. I know many people feel embarrassed to get help or feel like praying should be enough. I also know many feel uncomfortable talking to a stranger who doesn't know you or the whole story. However, I can tell you from lots of firsthand experience that counseling is one of the best things I have ever done. First, there is no shame in getting help. Yes, prayer is awesome, and the Spirit is there to be your Helper (John 14:26), but sometimes it is best to listen to that very same Spirit who is leading you to talk to a professional whom He has gifted. They have studied and have much experience in helping others through grief. Also, it will feel slightly uncomfortable because you don't know them and they don't know the whole story, but oftentimes the fact that they are unbiased and don't know all the details helps them to look at the situation with a clearer perspective than those closer to the situation.

If you are ready to find a counselor but aren't sure how to do that, just ask around. Maybe you have a friend who is a counselor; see if he or she has any colleagues to recommend. Or text some of your closest friends and ask if they've seen anyone before or know of any friends who have a counselor they like. Finding a counselor can be a hard thing to do. I joke that finding a good therapist can be as hard as finding a spouse! So if you can find someone who your network has already approved, that will help. Most insurances cover therapy. So you can check with your insurance provider too. And many therapists have websites now where you can check them out before calling. I would highly recommend seeing a therapist who is a believer, and you are welcome to ask this when you call to schedule an appointment.

BIBLICAL TRUTH ABOUT GRIEF

The Bible talks a lot about grief. One story about grief in particular is the one that opened my eyes to the humanity of Christ. After hearing it for the first time, I came to believe in Jesus!

> Now a certain man was ill, Lazarus of Bethany, the village of Mary and her sister Martha. It was Mary who anointed the Lord with ointment and wiped his feet with her hair, whose brother Lazarus was ill. So the sisters sent to him, saying, "Lord, he whom you love is ill." But when Jesus heard it he said, "This illness does not lead to death. It is for the glory of God, so that the Son of God may be glorified through it."
>
> Now Jesus loved Martha and her sister and Lazarus. So, when he heard that Lazarus was ill, he stayed two days longer in the place where he was. Then after this he said to the disciples, "Let us go to Judea again." The disciples said to him, "Rabbi, the Jews were just now seeking to stone you, and are you going there again?" Jesus answered, "Are there not twelve hours in the day? If anyone walks in the day, he does not stumble, because he sees the light of this world. But if anyone walks in the night, he stumbles, because the light is not in him." After saying these things, he said to them, "Our friend Lazarus has fallen asleep, but I go to awaken him." The disciples said to him, "Lord, if he has fallen asleep, he will recover." Now Jesus had spoken of his death, but they thought that he meant taking rest in sleep. Then Jesus told them plainly, "Lazarus has died, and for your sake I am glad that I was not there, so

that you may believe. But let us go to him." So Thomas, called the Twin, said to his fellow disciples, "Let us also go, that we may die with him."

Now when Jesus came, he found that Lazarus had already been in the tomb four days. Bethany was near Jerusalem, about two miles off, and many of the Jews had come to Martha and Mary to console them concerning their brother. So when Martha heard that Jesus was coming, she went and met him, but Mary remained seated in the house. Martha said to Jesus, "Lord, if you had been here, my brother would not have died. But even now I know that whatever you ask from God, God will give you." Jesus said to her, "Your brother will rise again." Martha said to him, "I know that he will rise again in the resurrection on the last day." Jesus said to her, "I am the resurrection and the life. Whoever believes in me, though he die, yet shall he live, and everyone who lives and believes in me shall never die. Do you believe this?" She said to him, "Yes, Lord; I believe that you are the Christ, the Son of God, who is coming into the world."

When she had said this, she went and called her sister Mary, saying in private, "The Teacher is here and is calling for you." And when she heard it, she rose quickly and went to him. Now Jesus had not yet come into the village, but was still in the place where Martha had met him. When the Jews who were with her in the house, consoling her, saw Mary rise quickly and go out, they followed her, supposing that she was going to the tomb to weep there. Now when Mary came to where Jesus was and saw him, she fell at his feet, saying to him, "Lord, if you had been here, my brother would not have died." When Jesus saw her weeping, and the Jews who had come with her also weeping, he was deeply moved in his spirit and greatly troubled. And he said, "Where have you laid him?" They said to him, "Lord, come and see." Jesus wept. So the Jews said, "See how he loved him!" But some of them said, "Could not he who opened the eyes of the blind man also have kept this man from dying?"

Then Jesus, deeply moved again, came to the tomb. It was a cave, and a stone lay against it. Jesus said, "Take away the stone." Martha, the sister of the dead man, said to him, "Lord, by this time there will be an odor, for he has been dead four days." Jesus said to her, "Did I not tell you that if you believed you would see the glory of God?" So they took away the stone. And Jesus lifted up his eyes and said, "Father, I thank you that you have heard me. I knew that you always hear me, but I said this on account of the people standing around, that they may believe that you sent me." When he had said these things, he cried out with a loud voice, "Lazarus, come out." The man who had died came out, his hands and feet bound with linen strips, and his face wrapped with a cloth. Jesus said to them, "Unbind him, and let him go." (John 11:1–44)

Lazarus and his sisters, Mary and Martha, were friends of Jesus. Upon hearing that Lazarus had died, Jesus wept (v. 35). It says again in verse 38 that He was deeply moved after He arrived to the tomb. We understand this, don't we? How the reality of our situation can hit us again, bringing yet another wave of grief along with it. We see Jesus, the Son of God, show us that there is nothing wrong with grief or emotions.

Upon hearing this story for the first time, I finally got the Savior. I knew the gospel message, but this was my first time I saw the humanity and raw love of God for His people. We see in verse 33 that He was deeply moved by the grief of the sisters, and I felt like He might also be deeply moved by my feelings. One of the things that held me back from believing in God had been my pain over what He had allowed to happen in my life. I was so mad about it. I wrestled with the question so many do: "How could a good God allow so much that's not good at all?" When I read this story, I felt like I stepped into the shoes of Mary and Martha, and the Savior heard my questions and felt my pain, and He wept. He wasn't asking me to get over it or to suck it up. He wept. And then He "unbound" Lazarus from the very thing that was causing so much grief.

You see, Lazarus came out still all bound up and the people were commanded to unbind him. I'm sure that was pretty smelly and messy business—he had been dead for a few days! Even so, Jesus said to unbind him.

This is my hope for you—that you will be able to step out of the grave of your grief and, with the power of the Savior, raise to new life. My prayer is that you use some of the permissions in this chapter, some of the verses that follow, along with the leading of the Holy Spirit in your own life, to unbind you. I hate that you are dealing with grief. I can't take it away, but I hope this becomes part of raising what feels dead to new life again.

OTHER VERSES ON GRIEF

You have kept count of my tossings; put my tears in your bottle. Are they not in your book? (Ps. 56:8)

He heals the brokenhearted and binds up their wounds. (Ps. 147:3)

He was despised and rejected by men; a man of sorrows, and acquainted with grief; and as one from whom men hide their faces he was despised, and we esteemed him not. (Isa. 53:3)

"Blessed are those who mourn, for they shall be comforted." (Matt. 5:4)

Blessed be the God and Father of our Lord Jesus Christ, the Father of mercies and God of all comfort, who comforts us in all our affliction, so that we may be able to comfort those who are in any affliction, with the comfort with which we ourselves are comforted by God. For as we share abundantly in Christ's sufferings, so through Christ we share abundantly in comfort too. (2 Cor. 1:3–5)

Not that I am speaking of being in need, for I have learned in whatever situation I am to be content. I know how to be brought low, and I know how to abound. In any and every circumstance, I have learned the secret of facing plenty and hunger, abundance and need. I can do all things through him who strengthens me. (Phil. 4:11–13)

Count it all joy, my brothers, when you meet trials of various kinds, for you know that the testing of your faith produces steadfastness. And let steadfastness have its full effect, that you may be perfect and complete, lacking in nothing. (James 1:2–4)

"He will wipe away every tear from their eyes, and death shall be no more, neither shall there be mourning, nor crying, nor pain anymore, for the former things have passed away." (Rev. 21:4)

CHAPTER 17

SANTA AND THE EASTER BUNNY

This is a very opinionated topic, and one that I approach with great sensitivity. Here's what I can tell you: regardless of which side you stand on today or choose to stand on in future years—you will both love and regret whatever you decide to do. You will think you have made the right decision and then doubt it one hundred times over.

How is that for encouraging? I say most of that in jest—well, in half jest—because the truth is it's going to be okay whatever you decide to do.

I have really great friends who wildly love Jesus, who stand strongly on both sides of this debate. I have friends who were raised to believe in Santa, who now don't raise their kids to put out milk and cookies for Ole' St. Nick. I have friends whose parents refused to lie to them about Santa and now sprinkle glitter in the front yard with their kiddos to make sure the reindeer don't miss their house this year. What I've learned is everyone turns out okay . . . as okay as any of us turned out (ha!).

There are lots of examples on how to do Santa and the Easter Bunny, so I'm not going to share that perspective with you today.

Where I struggled to find real help was how to not do Santa without being one of *those* Christians.

For me, choosing to not do Santa and the Easter Bunny didn't have anything to do with lying to my kids. I never felt upset with my parents for lying to me about Santa or the Easter Bunny, except for the one devastating day I realized Santa wasn't real after all. I remember sitting on the front porch of our home having just found every letter I had ever written Santa stashed away in my mom's dresser drawer. I asked her why she had the letters I wrote Santa and it all started to click. She told me I was right, that he wasn't real but just make-believe. Then it continued to click: none of them were real. Santa, the Easter Bunny, and the Tooth Fairy were all pretend. It was a hard afternoon on those front steps. After that day, there wasn't a smidge of bitterness. I happily joined the team to help all the littles believe. The magic of this jolly old man was now something I didn't believe in, but I was now able to help spread the magic to others. I never saw it as lying, rather a giant game of make-believe. I am a full supporter of anything we can do to instill creativity in our kids.

The loss of the magical game of make-believe is something I grieved a little for my kids when we decided to not do Santa or any other make-believe holiday character. To be completely honest, it wasn't until this past year that I felt completely sure we had made the right choice for our family. So, if you feel uncertain about what is best, know that you may not ever feel 100 percent sure you've made the right choice—because I'm not sure there is a right choice. Like most parenting decisions, we have to make the best one for our family at that time.

The deciding factor for me was *time*—I didn't feel like I could give my kids a full experience for both Advent and Santa without them missing out on both. On top of that, as I already shared at the beginning of the book, I felt like there was consistent talk from others about constantly trying to re-create the way things felt magical in our childhood, when we believed in Santa. They would tell me that the only seasons where the magic even remotely compares is when you have your own children, and then your children have children. That just sounded so sad to me. I was determined to help our family find as much magic in the real meaning of Christmas as many find in a jolly old man and a sleigh full of toys.

So we decided to not play make-believe with our kids when it comes to Santa Claus and the Easter Bunny (and the Tooth Fairy, for that matter), and our kids hate us for it. I'm kidding. My kids are obsessed with the holidays and don't know any different. (But like I've said, I have plenty of friends whose kids do believe and they love the holidays and Jesus just as much as we do.)

To keep things easier in this chapter, I'm going to focus on how we approach Santa, for the most part. This will keep me from having to say "Santa, the Easter Bunny, and the Tooth Fairy" every single time. I'm going to focus on Santa because it is a bigger topic, but obviously this approach is toward all holiday make-believe characters.

IF YOU DON'T WANT TO DO SANTA, HERE ARE SOME TIPS TO HELP MAKE THAT WORK BETTER FOR YOU

Focus on the Sacred Things with Your Kiddos

In each holiday chapter, there is a section for ways to make each holiday more sacred for kiddos. Focus on implementing those things instead of spending so much time building up the make-believe story. Show them how to find whimsy in what is true.

Train Your Child to Not Mess It Up for Other Kids

This is honestly one of my biggest fears, that my kid will be the one to ruin it for other kids. Like I've said, we don't think it's a bad thing and I do not want to take that magic away from another family. One of the ways we haven't ruined it for other kids is we don't really talk about Santa with our littlest and we train the older ones with what to say about Santa.

Until they are able to easily talk with us, ages three or four, we don't really even discuss Santa. Around that age and younger, it's hard to keep them from blurting out the truth about Santa to everyone at preschool. We keep him a non-issue, so he isn't something they discuss with kids. We don't over-share that he isn't real, but we also don't promote him either.

Once they are able to have a real conversation (we start around age four), we begin the conversation about Santa not being real. Again, before this, they never believed he was real because we didn't build him up at all. We talk through how others believe that he is real, but that it's not up to us to tell them he isn't—that's their parents' jobs. Basically, it's the same conversation parents have with their kids who once believed and now don't. After all, nobody wants to be a snitch!

Have some practice conversations with your kids, pretending to talk about Santa with friends. Help them find the best responses and keep having practice dialogues until you feel they understand.

Give Your Kids an Answer to the Ever-Popular Question: "What Are You Asking Santa to Bring You for Christmas?"

They will be asked this question one million times, so help them form an answer to this question ahead of time. I tell my kids when people ask this question, it's just their way of asking kids what they want for Christmas. As I've said before, we don't really make wish lists for Christmas, but who doesn't have a wish list going in the head all the time? We don't want to ever make someone feel uncomfortable by the fact that we don't do Santa. I find it's always better to foster connections with people, rather than to go into a detailed explanation of why we don't do Santa. So help your kid know how to respond to that question without making that person feel bad for asking.

Teach Them the Truth about St. Nicholas

We have some friends who choose to not bring in any part of Santa. They go so far as keeping all Santa decorations or even watching movies about Santa out of their house. While we don't pretend about Santa, we love St. Nicholas at our house. My girls have taken a picture with Santa every single year, we have an inflatable Santa roasting marshmallows with his reindeer in our front yard, and we have at least ten Santa hats in our house. This was important to me that my kids didn't get weird and awkward over the idea of Santa because, let's face it, he is everywhere at Christmas time and everyone talks about him to kids. Plus, the story of St. Nicholas is a really cool one!

The most helpful tool for teaching my kids about St. Nicholas is the DVD, *Buck Denver Asks . . . Why Do We Call It Christmas?* This has taught my girls, and Chris and me, so much about the real story of Christmas and St. Nicholas.

Because of this, we still do stockings as a reminder of what St. Nicholas did . . . plus they are just too much fun! One thing we added in the stocking this year to pay tribute to St. Nicholas was a bag of gold (chocolate) coins. When the girls pulled them out, we asked the girls why they were in their stockings, and they were able to tell us the whole story of St. Nicholas throwing a bag of coins into the home of a poor family to help them and it landing in their stockings. We celebrate him because he is a beautiful model of generosity.

Less Books and Movies with Santa

Especially when they are younger, and don't quite understand yet, we don't do many movies or books that have the make-believe Santa in it. Our one exception is the movie *Elf* because it's the best Christmas movie of all time. I've found that those movies and books just reinforce what I'm trying not to teach. No worries, there are plenty of Christmas books and movies to watch and read!

THOUGHTS ON THE EASTER BUNNY SPECIFICALLY

I would recommend to limit or choose not to do the Easter Bunny and baskets. As I've said with all of this, each family has to make their own decision on this issue. However, I would take some time to consider what you want this holiday to be about as a family. You can certainly still celebrate Jesus while maintaining the Easter

Bunny and egg hunt traditions; there is nothing wrong with that. However, make sure you aren't putting more energy into teaching your kids about the Easter Bunny than the story of the One who died for their sins and rose from the dead! That story is amazing enough on its own! If you do decide to do the Bunny and baskets, I would encourage you to limit how many things they get in the basket. Or maybe make them things that would encourage their hearts to worship God—like an age-appropriate Bible, kids devotional, journal, or something along those lines. And if introducing a new Bible or devotional isn't the need in your child's life at the time, perhaps you could replace a basket of gifts with growing or planting something that will visibly come to life over time. After all, Easter is about Jesus coming to life! Regardless of what you decide to do, just spend some time thinking through what you want this holiday to be about for your kids and what you want them to remember when they think back to this holiday.

FINALLY, WHAT TO DO WITH THE ELF ON THE SHELF?

Leave him on the shelf . . . at the store. We can agree to disagree on this issue and still be friends, deal? But if our aim is to teach our kids to be focused on celebrating Jesus' coming and being generous to others, our focus should simply not be on them behaving so they can get more things. We don't need to bribe our kids to obey us; this is something we should be working toward all the time (even though it is a struggle that is so very real).

With that said, if you are a family who simply has a ton of fun with the Elf on the Shelf, putting him in fun places each day, with a focus more on the hilarity of it and less on "the elf is watching you," then please play on. Or if there's another way to incorporate the same idea without the bribery part, then enjoy!

DO WHAT'S BEST FOR YOUR FAMILY

I shared my perspective, but this is what we've decided is best for our family. I didn't share much about the other perspectives only because I think those are pretty commonly done.

I'm going to end this chapter the same way I started it. This is a very opinionated topic, and one that I approach with great sensitivity. Here's what I can tell you: regardless of which side you stand on today or choose to stand on in future years—you will both love and regret whatever you decide to do. You will think you have made the right decision and then doubt it one hundred times over.

What we know for certain is that God is good (Ps. 119:68), and He loves you and your child (John 3:16). Often as parents we can stress out about things that aren't as big as we make them out to be. This is one of those things. I can tell you with full confidence that God sees your heart's intention and He delights in that because He delights in you (Zeph. 3:17). So, don't worry over this decision because it isn't one with a clear answer. Trust your Father and know that He chose you to be your kid's parent.

I love the New Living Translation of Proverbs 16:33, "We may throw the dice, but the LORD determines how they fall." Your Father has all this in His hands. If Jesus is the founder and perfector of our faith (Heb. 12:2), then I feel certain He can write and perfect the way you do holidays for your family. Trust Him and trust Him in you. You got this because He has you—and your kiddo—in the palm of His hands (Isa. 49:16)!

CHAPTER 18

P.S.: BE YOURSELF AND BE WITH OTHERS

We started with a desire to have our holidays made sacred—holy and set apart—by acknowledging that we all have regrets and wish there were a better way. I hope you've found that better way by noting the baby steps presented throughout this book, taking a few steps, and finding your own footing as you've gone along.

As we wrap up our time together, I want to encourage you with two things:

First, be yourself. After reading a book like this, we can fall back into a check-the-list mentality. Don't do that. We can also get on social media and start searching #sacredholidays and maybe see many ways of others "doing things better" than what you might have done. Hear me clearly: that is a lie. You be you. Take the ideas from this book before the Lord and let that be your starting place. And then go to those open spaces and let the Lord lead you down the particular path He wants for your holidays. Know this will change over the years as you learn better ways, or simply as life's surroundings change. But don't let the enemy have a voice in telling you that your way isn't very good. Baby steps, remember to take baby steps. Find the ways God wants *you* to season *your* holidays, not the way others are seasoning theirs.

Second, be with others. You weren't ever meant to live in isolation. Get your friends together and start a book club, text thread, or a private Facebook group and share your ideas with one another. Think of it as a realistic Pinterest thread, where the goal isn't to compare with each other, but grow with each other instead! None of us have this thing figured out, but together, we can come up with some really great ideas. And together we actually have a chance at doing them! There are two ways to join the greater Sacred Holidays community, beyond your in-person community, as seen below. We'd love to hear your journey, your ideas, and your voice!

- Share on social media and using #sacredholidays and tagging @sacredholidays. This will make it easier for your larger community (that's all of us!) to connect with, learn from, and encourage you. So as you try things listed here, or things you've come up with, be sure to tag the post up so we can all continue growing!
- We have a private Facebook group that allows you to connect easily with one another. This is your space to share what you want to share. I'd love for you to join: facebook.com/groups/ SacredHolidaysTribe.

I am so honored that you have trusted me with your time, all the way to this very last page. My biggest prayer for you is the same as it was at the beginning of this book from Isaiah 43:1–21. I will continue to ask that He, your good Father, would do a new work in you as you declare His praise! And remember, holidays aren't the only thing sacred; you are sacred, too. He sees you as holy and set apart!

ACKNOWLEDGMENTS

Writing a book has been the wildest thing I've ever done. It was just a year and a half ago that I even had the courage to say out loud that I wanted to write a book. And believe it or not, I said even then that I wanted it to be with B&H/LifeWay.

So my first thank-you goes to Camp Well and Jenn and Kelly for creating a space for me to dream with greater faith and courage than I had ever dared for myself. That was where the dream first started, but there are many to give credit to—it takes a village!

Chris, this acknowledgment and the dedication section of this book simply aren't enough. You are the greatest partner, my very best friend, a rockstar hubby, and a constant cheerleader. Thank you for knowing the realest version of me, and still loving and believing in me more than anyone else. You are the truest person I've ever known. I would choose you all over again, and I choose you again today. I love you, a lot a lot.

My girls: Karis, Moriah, and Chandler. You are one of the biggest reasons I write and teach, and sometimes, the biggest reason I stop writing and teaching. I want you to know that you can't do everything nor anything (no matter what our world might tell you), but you can do the very thing God has called you to do. I want you to run after Him and love Him with such wild faith and freedom, and to know what it means to choose Him over all the chaos of this world. Being your mom is more impor- tant to me than having my name on the back of this book, and I would choose you over any of this. Also, Mommy owes you a home-cooked meal (and should also acknowledge Chick-fil-A for providing sustenance for my family the past few months).

To all my extended family, who first taught me to love the holidays, but also to love God and others. Nils Smith, where would I be if you hadn't believed in me enough to share the Truth with me? Brother, you were the first great hero of my story, and I'm so very grateful for our friendship. Mom, you have a way of celebrating others and making the smallest things special. Dad and Robin, I have you to thank for giving me a great love for the sacred holidays. Tammy, Larry, and Kurt, thank you for inviting me into your family and all its traditions.

To all my friends, thank you for being my people. You have laughed with me, cried with me, celebrated with me, and prayed with me as I've ridden this rollercoaster. Erin Stearns, Kelley Ramsey, Kellye Skaer, Cheryl Butler, Marianne Schrank, and Tia Plum, thank you for being my people. On the days when I've felt I wasn't cut out for this, you held me up and spoke hope into me. And on the days that I needed to geek out with joy over signing a book deal, you were there jumping up and down with me! Church Project, especially our House Church and Tuesday Night Women's Bible Study, I adore you so much. Thank you for pushing me to love Jesus and His Word. Kat Armstrong, you have pushed, sharpened, and encouraged me since I was seventeen. Thank you for always seeing something in me and challenging me to go after it. Jamie Ivey, thank you for being such an amazing friend, coach, and cheerleader throughout this—it was so helpful to have someone who had been there and done that well. To my carpool crew, you make our street so fun . . . and you put up with all my "can we trade last-minute" requests with so much grace! I wouldn't want to live next-door to anyone else. There are so many more to thank, but for word count limits, I must stop here. But for all those that have pushed, prayed, and encouraged me, I am literally without words to share how thankful I am for you.

To my Sacred Holidays team and tribe, you were the inspiration for this entire project. Without you all, this book wouldn't exist. To my team, I'm so honored for how you give your time to love our people with your unique gifts. Kelly, Megan, Molly, Kellye, Cheryl, and Jordan, you are my dream team, and I can't wait to see what God does next and how He grows our team and this ministry! For all the long-time tribe members and all of those new to our little family, thank you for how you have gone all-in with our Facebook group (facebook.com/groups/ SacredHolidaysTribe) and also for how you have participated in all our studies and resources thus far. I can't wait for you to experience all the new things we will be unveiling. Connecting with you on social media is one of my favorites (@sacredholidays).

To Rachel and Blair Jacobson, of D.C. Jacobson & Associates, having you both as my literary agents has been such a gift. Thank you for taking a chance on this author with lots of ideas, dreams, and words. I'm so grateful for your guidance and cheerleading through this whole process. Thank you for working so hard on this book—here's to many, many more books and Bible studies to come!

LifeWay and B&H, I'm pretty sure I have said this in nearly every email exchange because this whole thing has never once lost its wonder on me. You have always been one of the greatest disciplers of my life. The books and studies you've published have been some of my greatest mentors. Thank you for inviting me into your family; it's been one of the great honors and joys of my life. A special thank-you to Mary Wiley, Ashley Gorman, and Devin Maddox for your encouragement, word polishing, patience, and absolute magic you work with all things publishing. You all are the real deal—you love Jesus, hold highly His truth, and steward words diligently. Thank you also to Beth Moore and the Living Proof Ministries team for hosting the LIT event and all the words you shared. Without your encouragement and hard truth that day, along with Jennifer Lyell's breakout session, I'm not sure I would've ever put the finishing touches on the book proposal I had swirling around in my head. Your honest advice that day was the confirmation I needed to do something.

And last but never least, Jesus. I've always thought it was strange when others acknowledged You in books, because it felt a bit forced and more for man than You. But now I get it—none of this would be without You. I have little to say apart from You. I hope these words bring You great glory, and cause women to choose more of You, Jesus!

> Now to him who is able to do far more abundantly than all that we ask or think, according to the power at work within us, to him be glory in the church and in Christ Jesus throughout all generations, forever and ever. Amen. (Eph. 3:20–21)

SACRED sh HOLIDAYS

For more #LessChaosMoreJesus resources, encouragement and connection, go to:

SACREDHOLIDAYS.COM

On social:
@sacredholidays
facebook.com/sacredholidays